math
expressions
Common Core

Dr. Karen C. Fuson

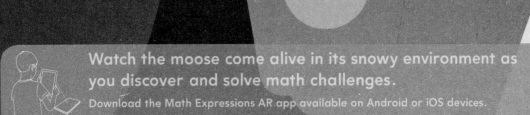

Watch the moose come alive in its snowy environment as you discover and solve math challenges.

Download the Math Expressions AR app available on Android or iOS devices.

Grade **3**

Volume 2

This material is based upon work supported by the
National Science Foundation
under Grant Numbers
ESI-9816320, REC-9806020, and RED-935373.

Any opinions, findings, and conclusions, or recommendations expressed in this material
are those of the author and do not necessarily reflect the views of the National Science Foundation.

Printed in the U.S.A.

ISBN 978-0-544-91981-5

3 4 5 6 7 8 9 10   0928   25 24 23 22 21 20 19 18 17

4500690407   B C D E F G

BIG IDEA 3 - Pictographs, Bar Graphs, and Line Plots

© Houghton Mifflin Harcourt Publishing Company

BIG IDEA 1 - Capacity, Weight, and Mass

BIG IDEA 2 - Analyzing Triangles and Quadrilaterals

Student Resources

Dear Family:

In this unit, your child will be introduced to fractions. Students will build fractions from unit fractions and explore fractions as parts of a whole.

Unit Fraction

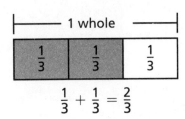

$$\frac{1}{3} + \frac{1}{3} = \frac{2}{3}$$

Fraction of a Whole

$\frac{3}{4}$ ← numerator
← denominator

Students will compare fractions with either the same denominator or the same numerator.

$$\frac{2}{6} < \frac{3}{6}$$

$$\frac{1}{2} > \frac{1}{6}$$

Students will also generate measurement data with halves and fourths of an inch such as hand spans and lengths of standing broad jumps and graph their data in a line plot.

You can help your child become familiar with these units of length by working with measurements together. For example, you might estimate and measure the length of something in inches.

Please contact me if you have any questions or comments.

Sincerely,
Your child's teacher

CCSS Unit 4 addresses the following standards from the Common Core State Standards for Mathematics: 3.NF.A.1, 3.NF.A.2, 3.NF.A.2.a, 3.NF.A.2.b, 3.NF.A.3, 3.NF.A.3.a, 3.NF.A.3.b, 3.NF.A.3.c, 3.NF.A.3.d, 3.G.A.2, 3.OA.A.3, 3.NBT.A.2, 3.MD.A.1, 3.MD.A.2, 3.MD.B.3, 3.MD.B.4, and all Mathematical Practices.

Estimada familia:

En esta unidad, se le presentarán por primera vez las fracciones a su niño. Los estudiantes formarán fracciones con fracciones unitarias y explorarán las fracciones como partes de un entero.

Fracción unitaria

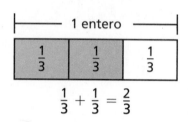

$$\frac{1}{3} + \frac{1}{3} = \frac{2}{3}$$

Fracción de un entero

$\frac{3}{4}$ ← numerador
← denominador

Los estudiantes compararán fracciones del mismo denominador o del mismo numerador.

$$\frac{2}{6} < \frac{3}{6}$$

$$\frac{1}{2} > \frac{1}{6}$$

Los estudiantes también generarán datos de medición con mitades y cuartos de pulgada, como palmos y saltos de longitud y graficarán sus datos en un diagrama de puntos. Puede ayudar a su niño a familiarizarse con estas unidades de longitud trabajando con medidas en conjunto. Por ejemplo, es posible estimar y medir la longitud de algo en pulgadas.

Si tiene alguna duda o algún comentario, por favor comuníquese conmigo.

Atentamente,
El maestro de su niño

© Houghton Mifflin Harcourt Publishing Company

CC SS En la Unidad 4 se aplican los siguientes estándares de los Estándares estatales comunes de matemáticas: 3.NF.A.1, 3.NF.A.2, 3.NF.A.2.a, 3.NF.A.2.b, 3.NF.A.3, 3.NF.A.3.a, 3.NF.A.3.b, 3.NF.A.3.c, 3.NF.A.3.d, 3.G.A.2, 3.OA.A.3, 3.NBT.A.2, 3.MD.A.1, 3.MD.A.2, 3.MD.B.3, 3.MD.B.4, y todos los de Prácticas matemáticas.

denominator	frequency table
elapsed time	horizontal bar graph
fraction	inch (in.)

A table that shows how many times each event, item, or category occurs.

Frequency Table	
Age	**Tally**
7	1
8	3
9	5
10	4
11	2

The bottom number in a fraction that shows the total number of equal parts in the whole.

Example:

$\frac{1}{3}$ ◄——— denominator

A bar graph with horizontal bars.

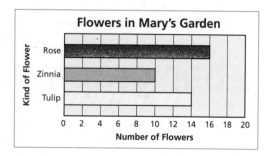

The time that passes between the beginning and the end of an activity.

A customary unit used to measure length.

12 inches = 1 foot

A number that names part of a whole or part of a set.

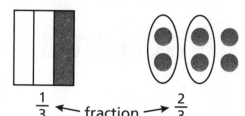

$\frac{1}{3}$ ◄— fraction —► $\frac{2}{3}$

key	mixed number
line plot	numerator
line segment	tally chart

A whole number and a fraction.

$1\frac{3}{4}$ is a mixed number.

A part of a map, graph, or chart that explains what symbols mean.

The top number in a fraction that shows the number of equal parts counted.

Example:

$\frac{1}{3}$ ←————— numerator

A diagram that shows frequency of data on a number line. Also called a *dot plot*.

A chart used to record and organize data with tally marks.

Tally Chart	
Age	Tally
7	I
8	III
9	IIII
10	IIII
11	II

A part of a line. A line segment has two endpoints.

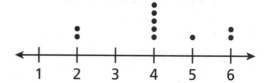

unit fraction

vertical
bar graph

A fraction whose numerator is 1. It shows one equal part of a whole.

Example:
$\frac{1}{4}$

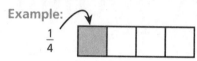

A bar graph with vertical bars.

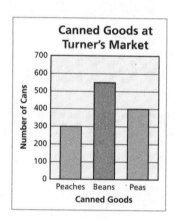

Fraction Rectangles

Cut out the bottom rectangle first.
Then cut on the dotted lines to make 4 rectangles.
Wait to cut out the top rectangle.

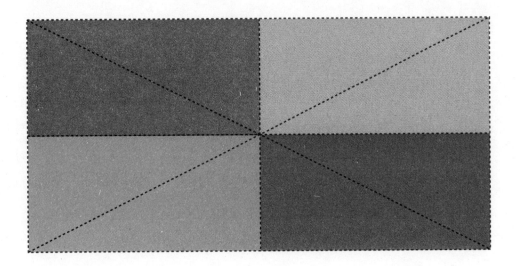

Understand Fractions

Name _____

Explore Unit Fractions

Use your rectangles from page 243A to make the whole shape. Count the equal parts. What unit fraction of the whole shape is one of the rectangles?

1

Number of equal parts _____   Unit fraction _____

2

Number of equal parts _____   Unit fraction _____

3

Number of equal parts _____   Unit fraction _____

© Houghton Mifflin Harcourt Publishing Company

Explore Unit Fractions (continued)

Use your triangles from page 243A to make a whole shape like the model shown. Count the equal parts in the whole. What unit fraction of the whole shape is the blue triangle?

4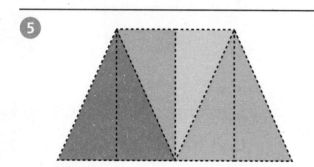

There are _____ equal parts in the whole shape.

The blue triangle is _____ of the whole shape.

5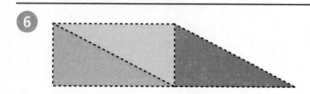

There are _____ equal parts in the whole shape.

The blue triangle is _____ of the whole shape.

6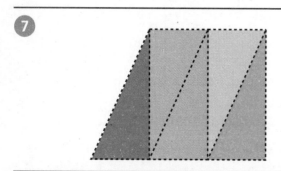

There are _____ equal parts in the whole shape.

The blue triangle is _____ of the whole shape.

7

There are _____ equal parts in the whole shape.

The blue triangle is _____ of the whole shape.

8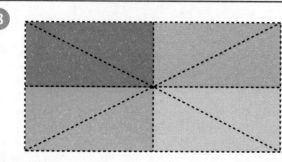

There are _____ equal parts in the whole shape.

One blue triangle is _____ of the whole shape.

© Houghton Mifflin Harcourt Publishing Company

Understand Fractions

Name _____

Unit Fractions and Fraction Bars

VOCABULARY
fraction
denominator
numerator
unit fraction

You can represent a **fraction** with a fraction bar. The **denominator** tells how many equal parts the whole is divided into. The **numerator** tells how many equal parts you are talking about.

1 whole

$\dfrac{1}{3}$ ← numerator
← denominator

Shade 1 part.

A **unit fraction** has a numerator of 1. Shade the rest of the fraction bars at the right below to represent unit fractions. What patterns do you see?

1 whole → Shade 1 whole. 1 one

Divide the whole into 2 equal parts. → Shade 1 part. $\dfrac{1}{2}$ one half

Divide the whole into 3 equal parts. → Shade 1 part. $\dfrac{1}{3}$ one third

Divide the whole into 4 equal parts. → Shade 1 part. $\dfrac{1}{4}$ one fourth

Divide the whole into 5 equal parts. → Shade 1 part. $\dfrac{1}{5}$ one fifth

Divide the whole into 6 equal parts. → Shade 1 part. $\dfrac{1}{6}$ one sixth

Divide the whole into 7 equal parts. → Shade 1 part. $\dfrac{1}{7}$ one seventh

Divide the whole into 8 equal parts. → Shade 1 part. $\dfrac{1}{8}$ one eighth

Build Fractions from Unit Fractions

Write the unit fractions for each whole. Next, shade the correct number of parts. Then show each shaded fraction as a sum of unit fractions.

9
Divide the whole into 5 equal parts.

→ Shade 2 parts.

$$\frac{1}{5} + \frac{1}{5} + \frac{1}{5} + \frac{1}{5} + \frac{1}{5}$$

$$\frac{1}{5} + \frac{1}{5} = \frac{2}{5}$$

10
Divide the whole into 3 equal parts.

→ Shade 2 parts.

11
Divide the whole into 7 equal parts.

→ Shade 5 parts.

12
Divide the whole into 8 equal parts.

→ Shade 7 parts.

13
Divide the whole into 6 equal parts.

→ Shade 3 parts.

✓ Check Understanding

A fraction bar is divided into 8 equal parts.
What unit fraction represents each part? _____.
Write an equation that shows 5 parts shaded.

© Houghton Mifflin Harcourt Publishing Company

Understand Fractions

Use Fraction Bars

Divide the fraction bar into unit fractions. Shade each fraction bar to show the fraction. Write the sum of the unit fractions under the shaded parts.

1 $\frac{1}{6}$

— 1 whole —

2 $\frac{2}{3}$

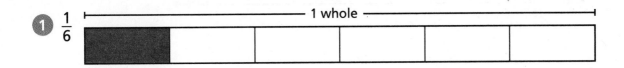

— 1 whole —

3 $\frac{7}{8}$

— 1 whole —

4 $\frac{2}{4}$

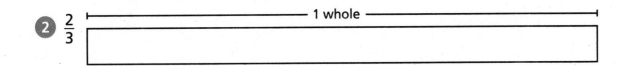

— 1 whole —

5 $\frac{5}{6}$

— 1 whole —

6 $\frac{3}{8}$

— 1 whole —

Content Standards **3.NF.A.1, 3.G.A.2**
Mathematical Practices **MP2, MP7**

Use Number Lines

First, divide each number line into the correct unit fractions. Then label each point. Show the target fraction by looping the unit fractions that make it.

7 $\frac{1}{6}$

8 $\frac{2}{3}$

9 $\frac{7}{8}$

0 ——————————————— 1

10 $\frac{2}{4}$

0 ——————————————— 1

11 $\frac{5}{6}$

0 ——————————————— 1

12 $\frac{3}{8}$

0 ——————————————— 1

© Houghton Mifflin Harcourt Publishing Company

✓ **Check Understanding**

Explain how Exercise 6 and Exercise 12 can both be used to show $\frac{3}{8}$.

Model Fractions

Name _____

Locate Fractions Less Than 1

Divide each number line into the correct unit fractions. Then label each point. Show the target fraction by looping the unit fractions that make it.

1 $\frac{1}{4}$

2 $\frac{1}{8}$

3 $\frac{3}{4}$

4 $\frac{5}{6}$

5 $\frac{2}{3}$

Plot the target fractions $\frac{2}{3}$ and $\frac{5}{6}$ on the number line below.

6

CC SS Content Standards **3.NF.A.2, 3.NF.A.2.a, 3.NF.A.2.b, 3.NF.A.3, 3.NF.A.3.c** Mathematical Practices **MP2, MP7**

Locate Fractions Greater Than 1

VOCABULARY
mixed number

Divide each number line into the correct unit fractions. Then label each point. Show the target fraction by looping the unit fractions that make it.

7 $\frac{5}{4}$

0   1   2

8 $\frac{8}{3}$

0   1   2   3

9 $\frac{5}{1}$

0 1 2 3 4 5 6 7 8 9 10

10 $\frac{6}{2}$

0   1   2   3   4   5

Introduce Mixed Numbers

A fraction greater than 1 that cannot be named as a whole number can be named as a mixed number. **Mixed numbers** have a whole-number part and a fraction part.

Examples of mixed numbers:

$1\frac{1}{2}$

$3\frac{2}{3}$

$4\frac{2}{4}$

Complete.

11 $\frac{5}{4} = \frac{4}{4} + \frac{1}{4}$

$= 1 + \frac{1}{4}$

$= \boxed{}$

$\frac{8}{3} = \frac{3}{3} + \frac{3}{3} + \frac{\boxed{}}{3}$

$= 1 + 1 + \boxed{}$

$= \boxed{}$

$\frac{8}{6} = \frac{\boxed{}}{6} + \frac{\boxed{}}{6}$

$= 1 + \boxed{}$

$= \boxed{}$

Locate Fractions on the Number Line

Find 1

Divide each number line into the correct unit fractions.
Label each point. Then locate 1 on the number line.

12

$\dfrac{1}{4}$

13

$\dfrac{1}{3}$

14

0

$\dfrac{2}{3}$

15

0

$\dfrac{9}{6}$

16

0

$\dfrac{11}{4}$

17 Explain how you located 1 for Exercise 15.

_____

_____

_____

Find Fractions

**Divide each number line into the correct unit fractions.
Then label each point. Use loops to show the target fraction.**

18 $\frac{3}{4}$

19 $\frac{5}{6}$

20 $\frac{3}{8}$

21 $\frac{5}{3}$

22 $\frac{1}{6}$

23 $\frac{10}{8}$

Check Understanding

Complete the sentence. The two fractions used to find 1

on the number line in Problem 23 are _____ and _____.

Locate Fractions on the Number Line

Name _____

Compare Unit Fractions with Fraction Bars

**The fraction bars are made up of unit fractions.
Look for patterns.**

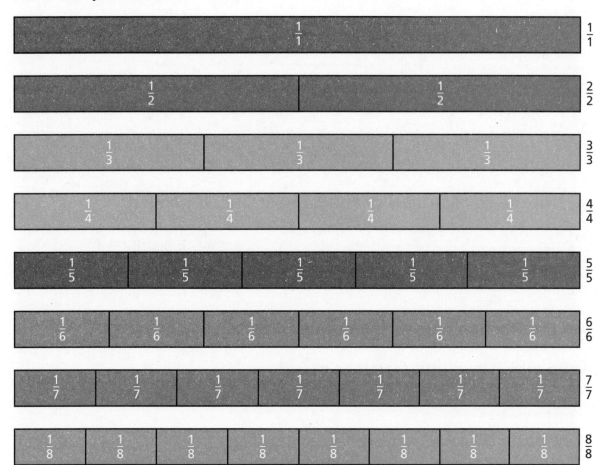

1. Describe two patterns that you see in the fraction bars.

_____

_____

_____

_____

Compare. Use <, >, or =.

2. $\frac{1}{3} \bigcirc \frac{1}{7}$

3. $\frac{1}{3} \bigcirc \frac{1}{2}$

4. $\frac{1}{6} \bigcirc \frac{1}{7}$

Compare Unit Fractions with Number Lines

The number line shows unit fractions.
Look for patterns in the number line.

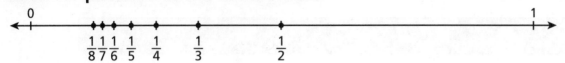

5 Describe a pattern that you see in the number line.

_____

_____

Compare. Use the fraction bars or the number line, if needed.

6 $\frac{1}{3}$ ◯ $\frac{1}{8}$ **7** $\frac{1}{4}$ ◯ $\frac{1}{2}$ **8** $\frac{1}{5}$ ◯ $\frac{1}{8}$

9 $\frac{1}{2}$ ◯ $\frac{1}{8}$ **10** $\frac{3}{7}$ ◯ $\frac{3}{4}$ **11** $\frac{5}{6}$ ◯ $\frac{5}{8}$

Solve. Use the fraction bars or the number line.

12 Between which two unit fractions is $\frac{1}{5}$ on

a number line? _____

13 Think about making a fraction bar for tenths.

a. How many unit fractions would be in the fraction bar? _____

b. How do you write the unit fraction? _____

14 Predict Can the fraction bars for any unit fractions
with even denominators always be split into
two equal parts? Explain your thinking.

_____

_____

**Check Understanding**
Draw a picture to show how you can compare $\frac{1}{6}$ and $\frac{1}{8}$.

© Houghton Mifflin Harcourt Publishing Company

Compare Unit Fractions

Name

Fraction Circles

Label each unit fraction.
Then cut out the fraction
circles on the dashed lines.

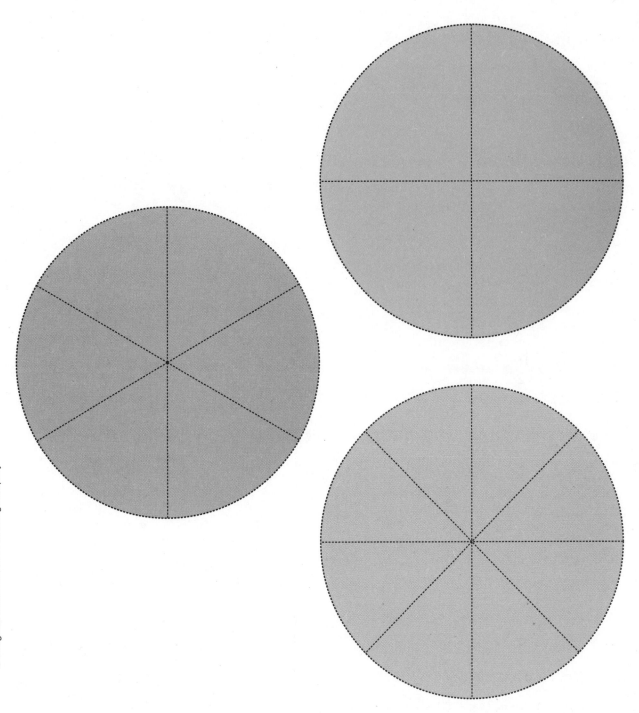

Compare Fractions

<u>Name</u>

Compare Fractions

Use these two circles as wholes.

Work with a partner. Use your fraction circles to compare fractions during the class activity.

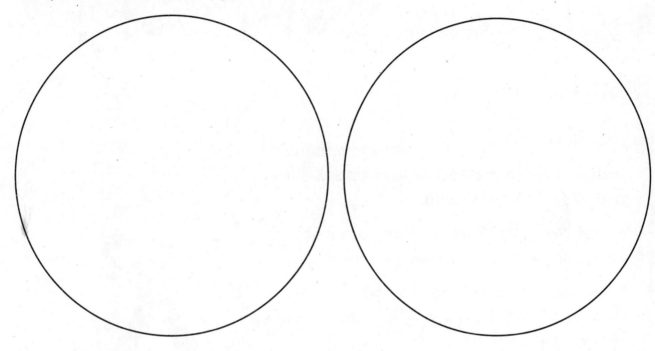

Record your work during the class activity.

1 $\frac{7}{8} \bigcirc \frac{5}{8}$ **2** $\frac{3}{6} \bigcirc \frac{5}{6}$

3 Explain how to compare two fractions that have the same denominator.

_____

_____

4 $\frac{3}{4} \bigcirc \frac{3}{8}$ **5** $\frac{5}{8} \bigcirc \frac{5}{6}$

6 Explain how to compare two fractions that have the same numerator.

_____

_____

Use Symbols to Compare Fractions

Compare. Use <, >, or =.

7 $\frac{2}{2} \bigcirc \frac{2}{3}$ **8** $\frac{1}{3} \bigcirc \frac{5}{3}$ **9** $\frac{3}{2} \bigcirc \frac{3}{6}$ **10** $\frac{5}{6} \bigcirc \frac{4}{6}$

11 $\frac{5}{8} \bigcirc \frac{3}{8}$ **12** $\frac{7}{3} \bigcirc \frac{7}{6}$ **13** $\frac{7}{8} \bigcirc \frac{3}{8}$ **14** $\frac{9}{4} \bigcirc \frac{9}{8}$

What's the Error?

Dear Math Students,

Today my teacher asked me to compare $\frac{3}{7}$ and $\frac{3}{9}$ and to explain my thinking.

I wrote $\frac{3}{7} = \frac{3}{9}$. My thinking is that both fractions have 3 unit fractions so they must be equal.

Is my work correct? If not, please correct my work and tell me what I did wrong. How do you know my answer is wrong?

Your friend,
Puzzled Penguin

15 Write an answer to Puzzled Penguin.

_____

_____

_____

 **Check Understanding**

Explain how comparing two fractions with the same denominator is different from comparing two fractions with the same numerator.

Compare Fractions

Name _____

Units of Length

Loop length units and fractions of units to show the length of the **line segment**. Write the length.

1

_____

2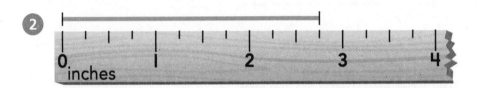

_____

3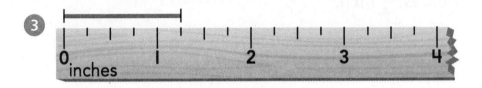

_____

4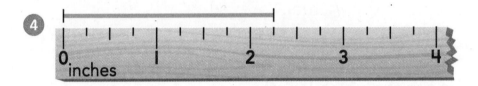

_____

5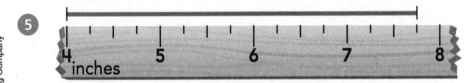

_____

6 Why is this ruler wrong?

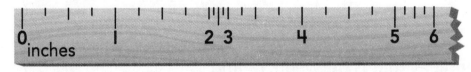

_____

© Houghton Mifflin Harcourt Publishing Company

Estimate and Measure Length

VOCABULARY
inch (in.)

inch

Estimate the length of each line segment in inches. Then measure it to the nearest $\frac{1}{2}$ inch.

7

Estimate: _____   Actual: _____

8

Estimate: _____   Actual: _____

Estimate the length of the line segment in inches. Then measure it to the nearest $\frac{1}{4}$ inch.

9

Estimate: _____   Actual: _____

Draw Line Segments

Draw a line segment that has the given length.

10 5 inches

11 $4\frac{1}{2}$ inches

12 $4\frac{3}{4}$ inches

13 Draw a line segment that is between $1\frac{1}{4}$ and $3\frac{3}{4}$ inches long. Trade books with a partner and measure the line segment they drew. _____

Customary Units of Length

Name

Line Plots with Fractions

VOCABULARY
line plot

A **line plot** shows the frequency of data on a number line. In science class, students measured the lengths of leaves in a leaf collection. They measured the lengths to the nearest $\frac{1}{4}$ inch. The line plot shows the results.

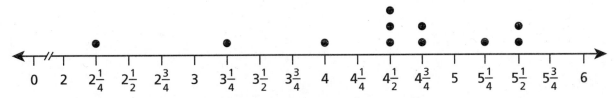

Length of Leaves (in inches)

Use the line plot to answer the questions.

14 How many leaves have a length of $4\frac{1}{2}$ inches? _____

15 How many leaves have a length that is less than 5 inches? _____

16 Write a question that can be answered using the line plot.

_____

_____

_____

_____

_____

Make a Line Plot

**Use the box below to record the actual measure for the line
segments that each classmate drew on page 258.**

[blank box]

17 Use the measurement data from the box above
to complete the line plot below.

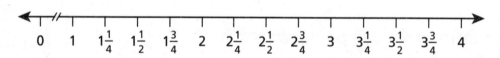

Length of Line Segments (in inches)

18 How many of the line segments have a

measure of $2\frac{1}{2}$ inches? _____

19 Which length appears the most often

on the line plot? _____

✓ Check Understanding

Describe how to measure a line segment to the
nearest $\frac{1}{4}$ inch.

© Houghton Mifflin Harcourt Publishing Company

Customary Units of Length

Show the shaded fraction as a sum of unit fractions.

1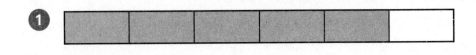

_____

Divide the fraction bar into the correct number of equal parts.

2 8 equal parts

```
┌─────────────────────────────────────────┐
│                                           │
└─────────────────────────────────────────┘
```

Shade the fraction bar to show the fraction. First divide the fraction bar into the correct unit fractions.

3 $\frac{1}{3}$

```
├────────────────── 1 whole ──────────────────┤
┌─────────────────────────────────────────────┐
│                                               │
└─────────────────────────────────────────────┘
```

Mark the number line to show the fraction. First divide the number line into correct unit fractions.

4 $\frac{5}{3}$

Compare. Use <, >, or =.

5 $\frac{1}{6}$ ◯ $\frac{1}{2}$

Name

Date

1 Flavien uses string in the colors and lengths shown below to create a pattern. Measure the length of each of the strings shown to the nearest $\frac{1}{4}$ inch.

2 Flavien uses 3 green strings, 2 blue strings, 4 red strings, and 2 yellow strings to make his pattern. Use the length measurements from the previous question to complete the line plot below.

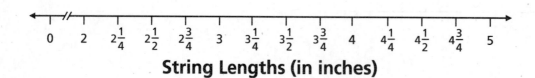

String Lengths (in inches)

Dear Family:

In math class, your child is beginning lessons about time. This topic is directly connected to home and community and involves skills your child will use often in everyday situations.

Students are reading time to the hour, half-hour, quarter-hour, five minutes, and minute, as well as describing the time before the hour and after the hour.

For example, you can read 3:49 both as minutes after the hour and minutes before the hour.

Forty-nine minutes after three   **Eleven minutes before four**

Students will be using clocks to solve problems about elapsed time.

Help your child read time and find elapsed time. Ask your child to estimate how long it takes to do activities such as eating a meal, traveling to the store, or doing homework. Have your child look at the clock when starting an activity and then again at the end of the activity. Ask how long the activity took.

Your child will also learn to add and subtract time on a number line.

If you have any questions or comments, please contact me.

Sincerely,
Your child's teacher

CC SS Unit 4 addresses the following standards from the Common Core State Standards for Mathematics: **3.OA.A.3, 3.NBT.A.2, 3.MD.A.1, 3.MD.A.2, 3.MD.B.3, 3.MD.B.4, 3.NF.A.1, 3.NF.A.2, 3.NF.A.2.a, 3.NF.A.2.b, 3.NF.A.3, 3.NF.A.3.a, 3.NF.A.3.b, 3.NF.A.3.c, 3.NF.A.3.d, 3.G.A.2,** and all Mathematical Practices.

Estimada familia:

En la clase de matemáticas su niño está comenzando lecciones que le enseñan sobre la hora. Este tema se relaciona directamente con la casa y la comunidad, y trata de destrezas que su niño usará a menudo en situaciones de la vida diaria.

Los estudiantes leerán la hora, la media hora, el cuarto de hora, los cinco minutos y el minuto; también describirán la hora antes y después de la hora en punto.

Por ejemplo, 3:49 se puede leer de dos maneras:

Las tres y cuarenta y nueve   **Once para las cuatro**

Los estudiantes usarán relojes para resolver problemas acerca del tiempo transcurrido en diferentes situaciones.

Ayude a su niño a leer la hora y hallar el tiempo transcurrido. Pídale que estime cuánto tiempo tomarán ciertas actividades, tales como comer una comida completa, ir a la tienda o hacer la tarea. Pida a su niño que vea el reloj cuando comience la actividad y cuando la termine. Pregúntele cuánto tiempo tomó la actividad.

Su niño también aprenderá a sumar y restar tiempo en una recta numérica.

Si tiene alguna pregunta o algún comentario, por favor comuníquese conmigo.

Atentamente,
El maestro de su niño

En la Unidad 4 se aplican los siguientes estándares de los Estándares estatales comunes de matemáticas: **3.0A.A.3, 3.NBT.A.2, 3.MD.A.1, 3.MD.A.2, 3.MD.B.3, 3.MD.B.4, 3.NF.A.1, 3.NF.A.2, 3.NF.A.2.a, 3.NF.A.2.b, 3.NF.A.3, 3.NF.A.3.a, 3.NF.A.3.b, 3.NF.A.3.c, 3.NF.A.3.d, 3.G.A.2, y todos los de** Prácticas matemáticas.

Name

Make an Analog Clock

Attach the clock hands to the clock face using a prong fastener.

Paper Clock

Name _____

Time to 15 Minutes

Write the time on the digital clock. Then write how to say the time.

1

2
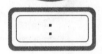

3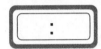
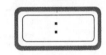

4

Write the time on the digital clock. Write two ways to say the time.

5

6

7

8

9

10

11

12

CC SS Content Standards **3.MD.A.1**
Mathematical Practices **MP5**

Show Time to 15 Minutes

Draw the hands on the analog clock. Write the time on the digital clock.

13 nine fifteen

14 half past seven

15 three o'clock

16 seven thirty

17 one forty-five

18 fifteen minutes after two

Times of Daily Activities

19 Complete the table.

Time	Light or Dark	Part of the Day	Activity
3:15 A.M.			
8:00 A.M.			
2:30 P.M			
6:15 P.M			
8:45 P.M			

Tell Time

Name _____

Time to 5 Minutes

Write the time on the digital clock. Then write how to say the time.

 20

[:]

_____

_____

21

[:]

_____

_____

22

[:]

_____

_____

 23

[:]

_____

_____

24

[:]

_____

_____

25

[:]

_____

_____

Write the time on the digital clock.

26 ten minutes after eight

[:]

27 seven twenty-five

[:]

28 eleven fifty

[:]

29 six forty

[:]

30 five minutes after three

[:]

31 four fifty-five

[:]

Time to 1 Minute

Write the time on the digital clock. Then write how to say the time.

32

```
[  :  ]
```

_____

_____

33

```
[  :  ]
```

_____

_____

34

```
[  :  ]
```

_____

_____

35

```
[  :  ]
```

_____

_____

36

```
[  :  ]
```

_____

_____

37

```
[  :  ]
```

_____

_____

Write the time on the digital clock.

38 ten fourteen

```
[  :  ]
```

39 fifty-two minutes after eight

```
[  :  ]
```

40 seven twenty-eight

```
[  :  ]
```

41 nine thirty-one

```
[  :  ]
```

✓ **Check Understanding**

Use your analog clock to show 1:26 and write the time in word form on your MathBoard.

Tell Time

Name _____

Times Before and After the Hour to 5 Minutes

Write the time as minutes *after* an hour and minutes *before* an hour.

1

_____
_____
_____
_____

2

_____
_____
_____
_____

3

_____
_____
_____
_____

4

_____
_____
_____
_____

5

_____
_____
_____
_____

6

_____
_____
_____
_____

7

_____
_____
_____
_____

8

_____
_____
_____
_____

9

_____
_____
_____
_____

Times Before and After the Hour to 1 Minute

Write the time as minutes *after* an hour and minutes *before* an hour.

(10)

(11)

(12)

_____

_____

_____

_____

(13)

(14)

(15)

_____

_____

_____

_____

✓ **Check Understanding**

Use the analog clock to show 7:31. Write the time
as minutes *after* the hour and minutes *before* the hour.

   _____

_____

Before and After the Hour

Name _____

Elapsed Time in Minutes and Hours

1 Find the end time.

Start Time	Elapsed Time	End Time
1:00 P.M.	2 hours	3:00
4:15 A.M.	4 hours	8:15
4:55 P.M.	18 minutes	5:13
2:15 A.M.	1 hour and 55 minutes	4:20
11:55 A.M.	2 hours and 17 minutes	2:22

2 Find the **elapsed time**.

Start Time	Elapsed Time	End Time
2:30 P.M.	2h. 12 min.	4:42 P.M.
7:45 A.M.	30 min.	8:15 A.M.
2:17 P.M.	5 h.	7:17 P.M.
11:00 A.M.	3 h.	2:00 P.M.
11:55 A.M.	4 h. 35 min	4:25 P.M.

3 Find the start time.

Start Time	Elapsed Time	End Time
1:17	3 hours	4:15 P.M.
2:30	15 minutes	2:45 P.M.
9:25	2 hours and 35 minutes	11:55 A.M.
2:22	1 hour and 20 minutes	3:42 A.M.

Solve Problems About Elapsed Time on a Clock

Solve. Use your clock if you need to.

Show your work.

4 Loretta left her friend's house at 3:45 P.M. She had been there for 2 hours and 20 minutes. What time did she get there?

_____

5 Berto spent from 3:45 P.M. to 4:15 P.M. doing math homework and from 4:30 P.M. to 5:10 P.M. doing social studies homework. How much time did he spend on his math and social studies homework?

_____

6 Ed arrived at a biking trail at 9:00 A.M. He biked for 1 hour and 45 minutes. He spent 20 minutes riding home. What time did he get home?

_____

7 Mario finished swimming at 10:45 A.M. He swam for 1 hour and 15 minutes. What time did he start?

_____

8 Eric has basketball practice from 3:30 P.M. to 4:15 P.M. He has violin practice at 5:30 P.M. Today basketball practice ended 30 minutes late and it takes Eric 15 minutes to walk to violin practice. Will he be on time? Explain.

_____

_____

✓**Check Understanding**

Explain how you could find the elapsed time between 3:15 P.M. and 4:45 P.M.

© Houghton Mifflin Harcourt Publishing Company

Elapsed Time

Name _____

Add Time

Solve using a number line. *Show your work.*

1 Keisha went into a park at 1:30 P.M. She hiked for 1 hour 35 minutes. Then she went to the picnic area for 45 minutes and left the park. What time did Keisha leave the park?

1:00   ↑   2:00   2:30   3:00   3:30   4:00

1:30 P.M.

2 Loren arrived at the children's museum at 1:15 P.M. First, he spent 30 minutes looking at the dinosaur exhibit. Next, he watched a movie for 20 minutes. Then he spent 15 minutes in the museum gift shop. What time did Loren leave the museum? How long was he in the museum?

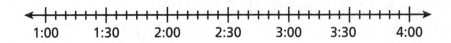

1:00   1:30   2:00   2:30   3:00   3:30   4:00

3 Caleb started working in the yard at 8:45 A.M. He raked for 1 hour 45 minutes and mowed for 45 minutes. Then he went inside. What time did he go inside? How long did he work in the yard?

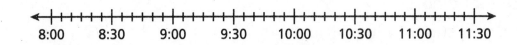

8:00   8:30   9:00   9:30   10:00   10:30   11:00   11:30

CC SS Content Standards **3.MD.A.1**
Mathematical Practices **MP1, MP4**

Subtract Time

Solve using a number line.   *Show your work.*

4 Hank finished bowling at 7:15 P.M. He bowled for
2 hours 35 minutes. At what time did he start bowling?

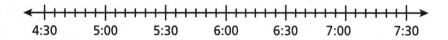

4:30   5:00   5:30   6:00   6:30   7:00   7:30

5 The school music program ended at 8:35 P.M. It lasted for
1 hour 50 minutes. What time did the program start?

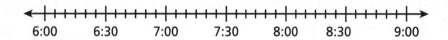

6:00   6:30   7:00   7:30   8:00   8:30   9:00

6 Lia served the salad at 3:15 P.M. It cooled in the refrigerator
for 35 minutes. She spent 15 minutes gathering the
ingredients from the garden and 15 minutes chopping
the vegetables. What time did Lia start working on
the salad?

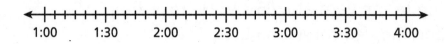

1:00   1:30   2:00   2:30   3:00   3:30   4:00

✓**Check Understanding**
Explain how you know to jump forward or
backward when adding and subtracting on the
number line.

Name _____

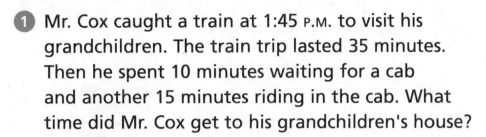

Make Sense of Word Problems Involving Time Intervals

Solve. Use a clock or sketch a number line diagram if you need to.

Show your work.

1 Mr. Cox caught a train at 1:45 P.M. to visit his grandchildren. The train trip lasted 35 minutes. Then he spent 10 minutes waiting for a cab and another 15 minutes riding in the cab. What time did Mr. Cox get to his grandchildren's house?

_____

2 Hirva left home at 9:45 A.M. and returned home at 11:20 A.M. She spent 55 minutes at the gym and the rest of the time at the library. How much time did Hirva spend at the library?

_____

3 Diego arrived at soccer practice at 8:45 A.M. Practice lasted 45 minutes and then it took him 10 minutes to walk home. What time did Diego get home?

_____

4 Jan started working on her homework at 6:25 P.M. and she finished at 7:30 P.M. She spent 45 minutes on a book report and the rest of the time on math. How long did Jan spend on math?

_____

5 Shanna finished her chores at 4:25 P.M. She spent 35 minutes cleaning her room, 20 minutes bathing her dog, and 15 minutes folding clothes. What time did Shanna begin her chores?

_____

What's the Error?

Dear Math Students,

Today I was asked to find the time Jim got to the doctor's office if he woke up at 7:55 A.M., spent 45 minutes getting ready, and then drove 20 minutes to the doctor's office.

Here is how I solved the problem.

From 7:55 on a clock, I counted up 45 minutes to 8:45, then I counted up 20 minutes to 9:05. Jim got to the doctor's office at 9:05 A.M.

Is my answer correct? If not, please correct my work and tell me what I did wrong. How do you know my answer is wrong?

Your friend,
Puzzled Penguin

6 **Write an answer to the Puzzled Penguin.**

_____

_____

_____

Solve.

7 Wayne left home at 3:50 P.M. to go to the park. It took 30 minutes to get to the park. He spent 45 minutes at the park. What time did he leave the park?

_____

✓ Check Understanding

Draw a number line to show Puzzled Penguin another way to find the time Jim arrived at the doctor's office.

Solve Word Problems Involving Time

Name _____ **Date** _____

Write the correct answer.

1 Write the time as minutes *after* an hour.

_____

2 Write the time as minutes *before* an hour.

_____

3 Carol leaves her house at 4:30 P.M. and drives for one hour to the grocery store. She shops for 20 minutes and then drives for one hour to get home. At what time does she get home?

Show your work.

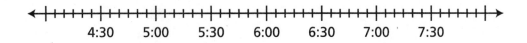

4:30   5:00   5:30   6:00   6:30   7:00   7:30

_____

4 Stephen leaves the house at 2:00 P.M. to walk the dog to the park. He walks for an hour. He lets the dog run around in the park for 50 minutes and then walks the dog home. He arrives home at 5:30 P.M. How long did it take Stephen to walk home?

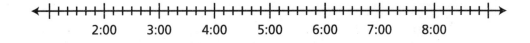

2:00   3:00   4:00   5:00   6:00   7:00   8:00

_____

5 Band practice starts at 3:15 P.M. and ends at 3:50 P.M. How long does practice last?

_____

Name _____ **Date** _____

PATH to FLUENCY

Add or subtract.

1 $14 + 23 = \boxed{}$ **2** $48 - 20 = \boxed{}$ **3** $27 + 11 = \boxed{}$

4 $56 - 32 = \boxed{}$ **5** $30 + 16 = \boxed{}$ **6** $49 - 43 = \boxed{}$

7
$$\begin{array}{r} 46 \\ +\ 25 \\ \hline \end{array}$$

8
$$\begin{array}{r} 42 \\ -\ 19 \\ \hline \end{array}$$

9
$$\begin{array}{r} 59 \\ +\ 18 \\ \hline \end{array}$$

10
$$\begin{array}{r} 60 \\ -\ 35 \\ \hline \end{array}$$

11
$$\begin{array}{r} 44 \\ +\ 38 \\ \hline \end{array}$$

12
$$\begin{array}{r} 74 \\ -\ 69 \\ \hline \end{array}$$

13
$$\begin{array}{r} 76 \\ +\ 19 \\ \hline \end{array}$$

14
$$\begin{array}{r} 91 \\ -\ 58 \\ \hline \end{array}$$

15
$$\begin{array}{r} 53 \\ +\ 47 \\ \hline \end{array}$$

Dear Family:

In the rest of the lessons in this unit, your child will be learning to show information in various ways. Students will learn to read and create pictographs and bar graphs. They will organize and display data in frequency tables and line plots. Students will also learn how to use graphs to solve real world problems.

Examples of pictographs, bar graphs, and line plots are shown below.

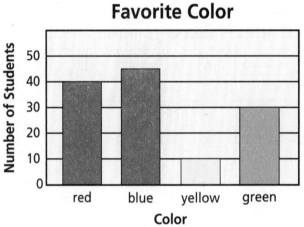

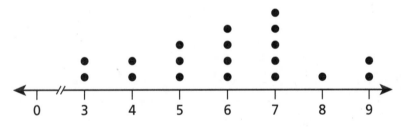

Number of Letters in a Name

Your child is learning how graphs are used in the world around us. You can help your child learn by sharing graphs that appear in newspapers, magazines, or online.

Thank you for helping your child learn how to read, interpret, and create graphs.

Sincerely,
Your child's teacher

Unit 4 addresses the following standards from the Common Core State Standards for Mathematics: **3.OA.A.3, 3.NBT.A.2, 3.MD.A.1, 3.MD.A.2, 3.MD.B.3, 3.MD.B.4, 3.NF.A.1, 3.NF.A.2, 3.NF.A.2.a, 3.NF.A.2.b, 3.NF.A.3, 3.NF.A.3.a, 3.NF.A.3.b, 3.NF.A.3.c, 3.NF.A.3.d, 3.G.A.2,** and all Mathematical Practices.

Estimada familia:

Durante el resto de las lecciones de esta unidad, su niño aprenderá a mostrar información de varias maneras. Los estudiantes aprenderán a leer y a crear pictografías y gráficas de barras. Organizarán y mostrarán datos en tablas de frecuencia y en diagramas de puntos. También aprenderán cómo usar las gráficas para resolver problemas cotidianos.

Debajo se muestran ejemplos de pictografías, gráficas de barras y diagramas de puntos.

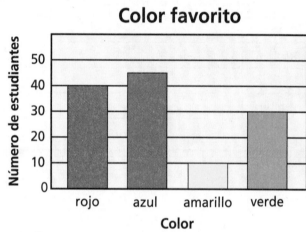

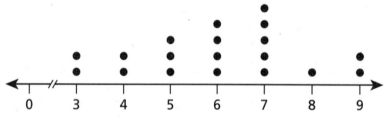

Número de letras en un nombre

Su niño está aprendiendo cómo se usan las gráficas en la vida cotidiana. Puede ayudarlo mostrándole gráficas que aparezcan en periódicos, revistas o Internet.

Gracias por ayudar a su niño a aprender cómo leer, interpretar y crear gráficas.

Atentamente,
El maestro de su niño

En la Unidad 4 se aplican los siguientes estándares de los Estándares estatales comunes de matemáticas: **3.OA.A.3, 3.NBT.A.2, 3.MD.A.1, 3.MD.A.2, 3.MD.B.3, 3.MD.B.4, 3.NF.A.1, 3.NF.A.2, 3.NF.A.2.a, 3.NF.A.2.b, 3.NF.A.3, 3.NF.A.3.a, 3.NF.A.3.b, 3.NF.A.3.c, 3.NF.A.3.d, 3.G.A.2, y todos los de** Prácticas matemáticas.

Read and Create Pictographs and Bar Graphs

Name _____

Read Bar Graphs

Look at this horizontal bar graph and answer the questions.

VOCABULARY
horizontal bar graph
vertical bar graph

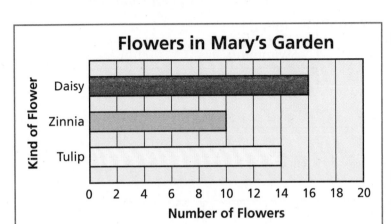

12 What do the bars represent?

_____

_____

13 How many tulips are in Mary's garden?

_____

Look at this vertical bar graph and answer the questions.

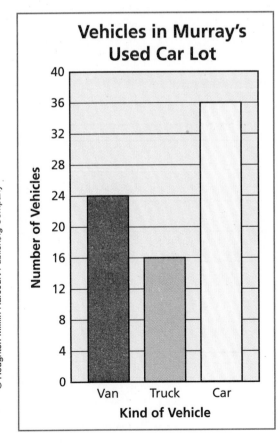

14 What do the bars represent?

_____

_____

_____

15 How many more vans than trucks are on Murray's Used Car Lot?

_____

Create Bar Graphs

16 Use the information in this table to complete the horizontal bar graph.

Favorite Way to Exercise	
Activity	Number of Students
Biking	12
Swimming	14
Walking	10

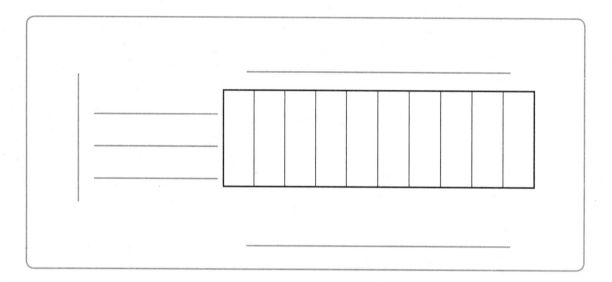

17 Use the information in this table to complete the vertical bar graph.

Favorite Team Sport	
Sport	Number of Students
Baseball	35
Soccer	60
Basketball	40

Read and Create Pictographs and Bar Graphs

Name _____

Solve Comparison Problems Using Data in Pictographs

Use the pictograph below to answer the questions.

What Musical Instrument Do You Play?	
🎸	♪ ♪ ♪ ♪ ♪
🥁	♪ ♪ ♪ ♪ ♪ ♪ ♪ ♪ ♪ ♪
🎹	♪ ♪ ♪ ♪ ♪ ♪ ♪
🎻	♪ ♪ ♪

Each ♪ = 4 students.

18 How many more students play guitar than violin?

_____

19 How many students do not play drums?

_____

20 Do more students play drums or guitar and violin combined?

_____

21 How many more students play guitar and piano combined than drums?

_____

22 Twelve fewer students play this instrument than drums.

_____

23 How many students in all were surveyed?

_____

Solve Comparison Problems Using Data in Bar Graphs

Use the bar graph below to answer the questions.

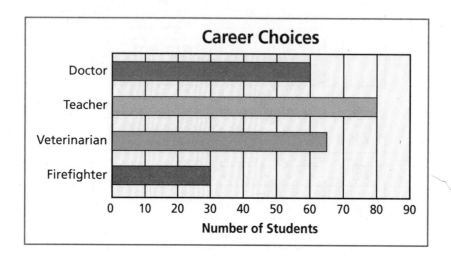

24 Twenty fewer students chose this career than teacher.

_____

25 Did more students choose veterinarian and firefighter combined or teacher?

_____

26 How many more students chose doctor than firefighter?

_____

27 How many students did not choose teacher?

_____

28 How many students in all were surveyed?

_____

29 How many more students chose doctor and firefighter combined than veterinarian?

_____

✓ Check Understanding

What equation can you write to solve Problem 27?

_____

Read and Create Pictographs and Bar Graphs

Name _____

Create Bar Graphs with Multidigit Numbers

13 Use the information in the table on the right to make a horizontal bar graph.

Joe's Cap Collection	
Type	Caps
Baseball	60
Basketball	35
Golf	20

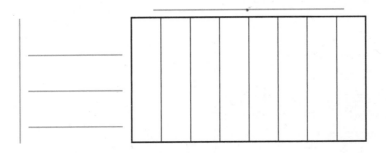

14 Use the information in the table on the right to make a vertical bar graph.

Summer Bike Sales	
Type of Bike	Number Sold
Road Bike	200
Mountain Bike	600
Hybrid Bike	450

Solve Problems Using Bar Graphs

Use the horizontal bar graph to answer the questions below.

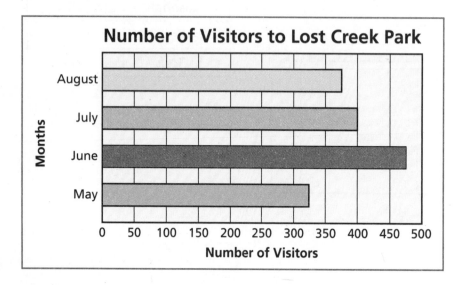

15 How many more visitors went to Lost Creek Park in June than in May?

_____

16 How many visitors did the park have during the months of May and June combined?

_____

17 How many more visitors went to the park in July than in August?

_____

18 Did more visitors go to the park in June or in May and August combined?

_____

Check Understanding

Suppose there were 225 visitors in September. Draw a bar graph that includes September.

Read and Create Bar Graphs with Multidigit Numbers

Name _____

Frequency Tables and Line Plots

VOCABULARY
tally chart
frequency table
line plot

The ages of some players on a basketball team can be shown in different ways.

A **tally chart** can be used to record and organize data.

A **frequency table** shows how many times events occur.

A **line plot** shows the frequency of data on a number line.

Tally Chart	
Age	Tally
7	I
8	III
9	IHII
10	IIII
11	II

Frequency Table	
Age	Numbers of Players
7	1
8	3
9	5
10	4
11	2

Line Plot

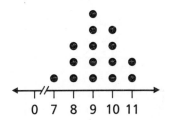

Ages of Basketball Players

Make Sense of Data Displays

Use the data displays above to answer Exercises 1–4.

1 How many basketball players are 10 years old?

_____

2 Which age appears the most often?

_____

3 Are there more players younger than 9 or more players that are older than 9?

_____

4 Write another question that can be answered by using the data displays.

_____

_____

Create Line Plots with Fractions

1 Have 10 classmates spread their fingers apart as far as possible, and measure from the tip of the thumb to the tip of the little finger to the nearest $\frac{1}{2}$ inch. Record the data in the tally chart below and then make a frequency table.

Tally Chart	
Length	Tally

Frequency Table	
Length	Number of Classmates

2 Use the data to make a line plot.

0

Hand Span Lengths (in inches)

3 Which length occurred the most often? _____

4 Write a question that can be answered by using the data in the line plot.

_____

_____

✓ Check Understanding

Complete. The line plot above shows that _____ students had a handspan _____ inches long.

Represent and Organize Data

© Houghton Mifflin Harcourt Publishing Company

Solve Problems Using a Bar Graph

Five teams of students are riding their bikes after school to raise money for the computer lab. Every completed mile will earn the computer lab $2. The bar graph below shows the number of miles completed in one week.

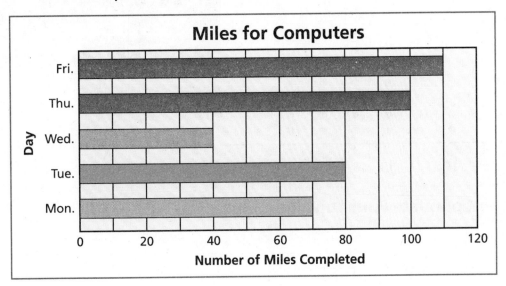

Use the bar graph to solve the problems.

1 How much money was earned for the computer lab on Tuesday?

_____

2 How many fewer miles were completed on Monday than on Friday?

_____

3 How many miles in all did the students ride?

_____

4 How many more miles did students ride on Monday and Tuesday combined than on Friday?

_____

5 There are 4 riders on each of the 5 teams. If each student completed the same number of miles, how many miles did each student ride on Wednesday?

_____

6 Did students ride more miles on Monday and Wednesday combined or on Thursday?

_____

_____

Solve Problems Using a Line Plot

The physical fitness coach asked her students to walk around a track four times. Four laps equal one mile. She recorded their times on the line plot below.

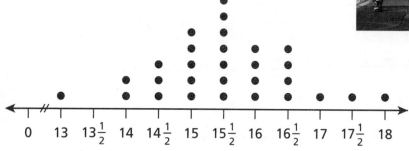

Time to Complete Four Laps (in minutes)

Use the plot to solve the problems.

7 What is the difference between the greatest and the least amount of time students took to walk four laps?

_____

8 Did more students complete the laps in 16 minutes or more or in $15\frac{1}{2}$ minutes or fewer?

_____

9 How many students completed four laps in 16 minutes?

_____

10 The coach recorded the times of how many students?

_____

11 How many students completed four laps in fewer than 15 minutes?

_____

✓ Check Understanding

Complete the sentences.
Most students completed the

laps in _____ minutes. The

_____ dots above that time

represent _____ students.

Use Graphs to Solve Time and Measurement Problems

<u>**Name**</u>

Math and Sports

Many students take part in a track and field day at school each year. One event is the standing broad jump. In the standing broad jump, the jumper stands directly behind a starting line and then jumps. The length of the jump is measured from the starting line to the mark of the first part of the jumper to touch the ground.

Complete.

1 Your teacher will tell you when to do a standing broad jump. Another student should measure the length of your jump to the nearest $\frac{1}{2}$ foot and record it on a slip of paper.

2 Record the lengths of the students' jumps in the box below.

© Houghton Mifflin Harcourt Publishing Company

How Far Can a Third Grader Jump?

To analyze how far a third grader can jump, the data needs to be organized and displayed.

3 Use the lengths of the students' jumps to complete the tally chart and the frequency table.

Tally Chart	
Length	**Tally**

Frequency Table	
Length	**Number of Students**

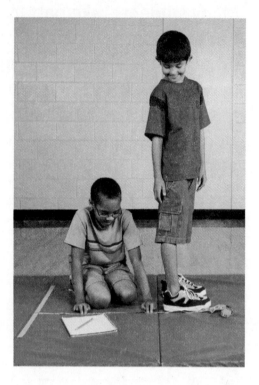

4 Make a line plot.

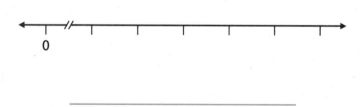

0

Focus on Mathematical Practices

1 Use the data in the table to complete the bar graph.

Students	
Grade	**Number of Students**
2nd	25
3rd	40
4th	80
5th	50

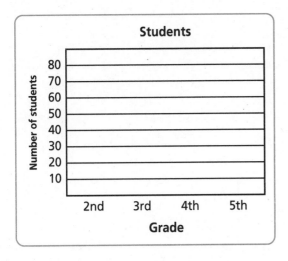

2 Use the data in the table to complete the line plot.

Time Spent at After School Activities	
Hours	**Number of students**
$\frac{1}{2}$	4
1	3
$1\frac{1}{2}$	2
2	1
$2\frac{1}{2}$	3
3	5

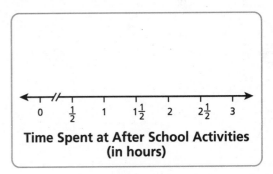

The animals that Gary saw while hiking are shown in the pictograph on the right. Use the pictograph to answer questions 3 and 4.

3 How many toads did Gary see?

_____

4 How many more frogs than turtles did Gary see?

_____

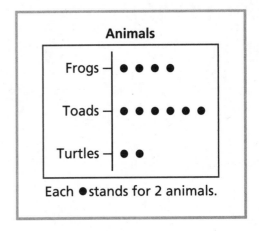

Name _____   Date _____

Multiply or divide.

1 $8 \div 2 =$ ☐

2 $3 \times 5 =$ ☐

3 $7 \times 6 =$ ☐

4 $4 \times 10 =$ ☐

5 $60 \div 10 =$ ☐

6 $7 \div 1 =$ ☐

7 $64 \div 8 =$ ☐

8 $6 \times 9 =$ ☐

9 $45 \div 5 =$ ☐

Add or subtract.

10
```
  342
+ 117
```

11
```
  754
- 342
```

12
```
  263
+ 474
```

13
```
  556
- 438
```

14
```
  387
+ 476
```

15
```
  803
- 598
```

1 Select the way that shows the shaded fraction.
Mark all that apply.

Ⓐ $\frac{1}{4}$

Ⓑ $\frac{4}{3}$

Ⓒ $\frac{3}{4}$

Ⓓ $\frac{1}{4} + \frac{1}{4} + \frac{1}{4}$

Ⓔ $\frac{4}{1} + \frac{4}{1} + \frac{4}{1}$

2 For numbers 2a–2d, choose Yes or No
to tell whether the words say the time
on the clock.

2a. twenty-six minutes before eleven   ○ Yes   ○ No

2b. thirty-four minutes after twelve   ○ Yes   ○ No

2c. thirty-four minutes after eleven   ○ Yes   ○ No

2d. twenty-six minutes before twelve   ○ Yes   ○ No

3 Use a straightedge to divide the fraction bar
into 6 equal parts. Then shade four parts.

|←——————————— 1 whole ———————————→|

What fraction does the shaded fraction bar represent?

_____

Show the fraction as the sum of unit fractions.

_____

4 Kyle starts his homework at 6:30 P.M. He spends 35 minutes doing math homework and 40 minutes doing science homework. At what time does Kyle finish his homework? How much time does he spend on homework? Use the number line to help you.

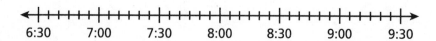

Kyle finishes his homework at _____ P.M.

He spends
| 1 hour 5 minutes |
| 1 hour 15 minutes | on homework.
| 1 hour 25 minutes |

5 Locate the fraction on the number line.

$\frac{3}{4}$

6 The bar graph shows the number of plants sold at a nursery.

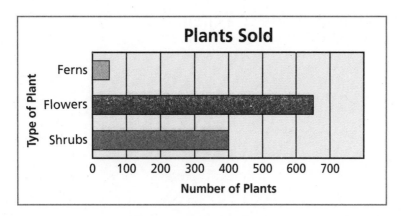

Plants Sold

Type of Plant

Ferns

Flowers

Shrubs

0   100   200   300   400   500   600   700

Number of Plants

How many more flowers does the nursery sell than ferns and shrubs combined?

_____ more flowers

Write and answer another question using data from the graph.

7 Estimate the length of the marker in inches. Then measure it to the nearest $\frac{1}{4}$ inch.

Estimate: _____ in.   Actual: _____ in.

8 Jeff has two shelves. The length of the wood shelf is $\frac{2}{4}$ meter and the length of the metal shelf is $\frac{2}{8}$ meter.

Which shelf is longer? Label and shade the circles to help solve the problem.

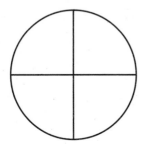   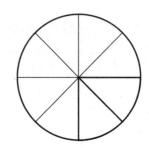

The _____ shelf is longer.

9 Tom measures the distances some softballs were thrown from home plate. The results are shown in the line plot. For numbers 9a–9d, select True or False for each statement.

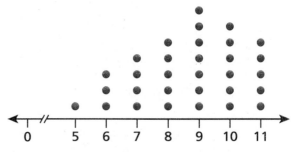

Distance from Home Plate (in feet)

9a. 8 softballs are thrown 5 feet.   ○ True   ○ False

9b. 13 softballs are thrown less than 9 feet.   ○ True   ○ False

9c. 11 softballs are thrown farther than 9 feet.   ○ True   ○ False

9d. 4 feet is the difference between the least and greatest distances thrown.   ○ True   ○ False

10 Use the data in the table to complete the pictograph and bar graph.

T-Shirt Sales			
Size	Small	Medium	Large
Number of Shirts	40	70	50

T-Shirt Sales

Small	
Medium	
Large	

Key: _____

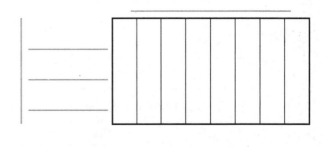

Which graph would you choose to show the data? Why?

11 Write the start time or end time to complete the chart.

8:48 A.M.   3:25 A.M.   12:50 P.M.

8:53 A.M.   3:35 P.M.   1:10 P.M.

Start Time	Elapsed Time	End Time
8:15 A.M.	38 minutes	
	55 minutes	4:20 A.M.
10:45 A.M.	2 hours 25 minutes	

⑫ Diane has $\frac{5}{4}$ meter of blue ribbon and $\frac{3}{4}$ meter of red ribbon. Write a comparison. Which ribbon is longer?

Comparison: _____

The _____ ribbon is longer.

⑬ The frequency table shows the lengths of some books in a classroom.

Part A

Use the frequency table to complete the line plot.

Frequency Table	
Length (in inches)	Number of Books
5	2
$5\frac{1}{2}$	3
6	6
$6\frac{1}{2}$	5
7	8
$7\frac{1}{2}$	5
8	7

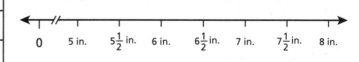

0   5 in. $5\frac{1}{2}$ in.   6 in. $6\frac{1}{2}$ in.   7 in. $7\frac{1}{2}$ in.   8 in.

_____

Part B

Most book lengths are between which two measures?

_____ inches and _____ inches

What if you measure three more book lengths at $7\frac{1}{2}$ inches and add the data to the line plot? How would your answer change?

© Houghton Mifflin Harcourt Publishing Company

Plan a School Festival

Imagine that your class is going to have a festival.
You have been asked to figure out how much juice it
takes to make 15 samples of a juice drink.

1 The table shows the amount of juice you need to make
5 and 10 samples of juice drink. Complete the table and graph.

Juice Drink	
Samples	**Milliliters**
5	250
10	500
15	

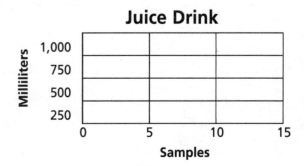

Juice Drink

2 Make a schedule for yourself on a sheet of paper.
Remember to include time to set up the video,
clean up after the festival, and take a 5-minute
break between activities.

Activity	Time
Watch a Video	35 minutes
Paint a Picture	30 minutes
Sing a Song	10 minutes
Eat Sandwiches	20 minutes
Make a Puppet	25 minutes

3 Write a good time for the festival to start. If it
starts at that time, at what time will it end?
Explain your thinking on your paper.

4 Making puppets took longer than planned on the schedule. This table shows the lengths of time that students spent making puppets.

Make a line plot to show the times.

Frequency Table	
Length of Time (in minutes)	Number of Students
25	2
26	5
27	3
28	7
29	3
30	9
31	1

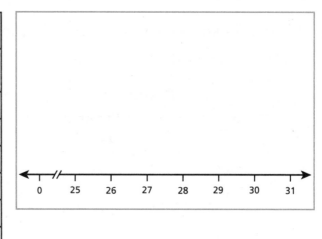

_____

The same activities will be done at next year's festival. Do you think more time should be allowed for puppet making next year? Explain.

5 The art teacher made a table to show the number of each type of painting students painted.

Make a pictograph to show the data from the table.

Frequency Table	
Subject of Painting	Number of Paintings
Animals	12
People	8
Places	7
Shapes or Designs	3

Types of Paintings	
Animals	
People	
Places	
Shapes/Designs	
Key: Each _____ = _____.	

Dear Family:

Your child is currently learning about perimeter and area. Students find the area of a rectangle by counting the number of square units inside the figure and find the perimeter of a rectangle by counting linear units around the outside of the figure. They develop methods to find the perimeter and area of a rectangle.

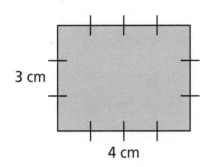

Perimeter = distance around the rectangle

Perimeter = *side length + side length +*
side length + side length

P = 4 cm + 3 cm + 4 cm + 3 cm

P = 14 cm

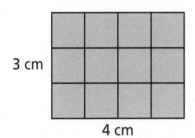

Area = square units inside the rectangle

Area = *side length × side length*

A = 4 cm × 3 cm

A = 12 sq cm

Students draw rectangles and discover relationships between perimeter and area, such as for a given area, the longest, skinniest rectangle has the greatest perimeter and the rectangle with sides closest to the same length or the same length has the least perimeter.

Students create shapes with tangrams and use the shapes as improvised units to measure area.

In this unit, students use fraction bars and number lines to find equivalent fractions and solve real world problems using their understanding of fraction concepts.

$$\frac{1}{2} = \frac{3}{6}$$

If you have any questions or comments, please contact me.

Thank you.

Sincerely,
Your child's teacher

CC SS Unit 5 addresses the following standards from the Common Core State Standards for Mathematics: 3.G.A.1, 3.G.A.2, 3.MD.C.5, 3.MD.C.5.a, 3.MD.C.5.b, 3.MD.C.6, 3.MD.C.7, 3.MD.C.7.a, 3.MD.C.7.b, 3.MD.C.7.c, 3.MD.C.7.d, 3.MD.D.8, 3.NF.A.2.a, 3.NF.A.2.b, 3.NF.A.3, 3.NF.A.3.a, 3.NF.A.3.b, 3.NF.A.3.c, and all Mathematical Practices.

Estimada familia:

Su niño está aprendiendo acerca de perímetro y área. Los estudiantes encontrarán el área de un rectángulo contando las unidades cuadradas que caben en la figura y hallarán el perímetro de un rectángulo contando las unidades lineales alrededor de la figura. Ellos desarrollarán métodos para hallar el perímetro y el área de un rectángulo.

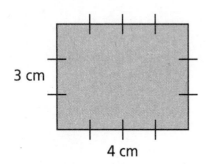

Perímetro = distancia alrededor del rectángulo

Perímetro = *largo del lado* + *largo del lado* + *largo del lado* + *largo del lado*

$P = 4$ cm $+ 3$ cm $+ 4$ cm $+ 3$ cm

$P = 14$ cm

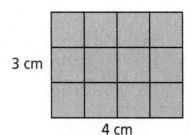

Área = unidades cuadradas dentro del rectángulo

Área = *largo del lado* × *largo del lado*

$A = 4$ cm $\times 3$ cm

$A = 12$ cm cuad

Los estudiantes dibujarán rectángulos y descubrirán cómo se relacionan el perímetro y el área, por ejemplo, para un área determinada, el rectángulo más largo y angosto tiene el perímetro mayor y el rectángulo con lados de igual o casi igual longitud, tiene el perímetro menor.

Los estudiantes crearán figuras con tangramas y las usarán como medidas improvisadas para medir área.

En esta unidad, los estudiantes usarán barras de fracciones y rectas numéricas para hallar fracciones equivalentes y resolver problemas cotidianos usando los conceptos que aprendan sobre fracciones.

$$\frac{1}{2} = \frac{3}{6}$$

Si tiene alguna duda o algún comentario, por favor comuníquese conmigo.

Atentamente,
El maestro de su niño

En la Unidad 5 se aplican los siguientes estándares de los Estándares estatales comunes de matemáticas: **3.G.A.1, 3.G.A.2, 3.MD.C.5, 3.MD.C.5.a, 3.MD.C.5.b, 3.MD.C.6, 3.MD.C.7, 3.MD.C.7.a, 3.MD.C.7.b, 3.MD.C.7.c, 3.MD.C.7.d, 3.MD.D.8, 3.NF.A.2.a, 3.NF.A.2.b, 3.NF.A.3, 3.NF.A.3.a, 3.NF.A.3.b, 3.NF.A.3.c, y todos los de** Prácticas matemáticas.

area

perimeter

decompose

unit square

equivalent
fractions

The distance around a figure.

Example:
Perimeter
= 3 cm + 5 cm + 3 cm + 5 cm = 16 cm

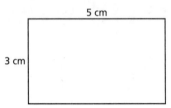

The total number of square units that cover a figure.

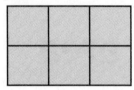

Example:
The area of the rectangle is 6 square units.

A square whose area is 1 square unit.

To separate or break apart (a geometric figure or a number) into smaller parts.

Fractions that name the same amount.

Example:

$\frac{1}{2}$ and $\frac{2}{4}$

equivalent fractions

Name _____

Recognize Perimeter and Area

VOCABULARY
perimeter
unit square

On this page, the dots on the dot paper are 1 cm apart. Use the rectangle for Exercises 1–4.

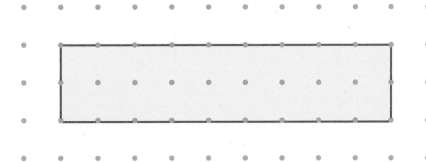

1 What part of the rectangle is its **perimeter**?

_____

2 What part of the rectangle is its area?

_____

3 Find the perimeter. Draw tick marks to help.

_____

4 Find the area. Draw **unit squares** to help.

_____

5 Draw a rectangle 4 cm long and 3 cm wide on the dot paper. Find the perimeter and area.

Perimeter _____

Area _____

6 Explain how you found the area of the rectangle in Exercise 5.

_____

_____

_____

_____

_____

_____

Content Standards 3.MD.C.5, 3.MD.C.5.a, 3.MD.C.5.b, 3.MD.C.6, 3.MD.C.7, 3.MD.C.7.a, 3.MD.C.7.b, 3.MD.D.8 Mathematical Practices MP2, MP5

Perimeter and Area **309**

Find Perimeter and Area

Find the perimeter and area of each figure.
Remember to include the correct units in your answers.

7 perimeter   area

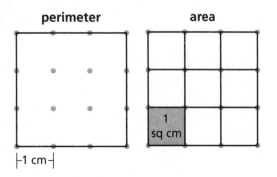

Perimeter = _____

Area = _____

8

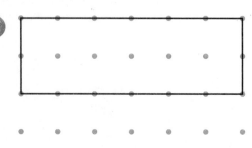

Perimeter = _____

Area = _____

9

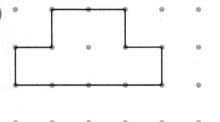

Perimeter = _____

Area = _____

10

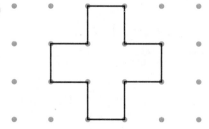

Perimeter = _____

Area = _____

11

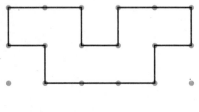

Perimeter = _____

Area = _____

12

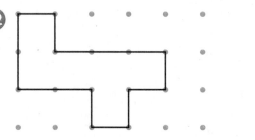

Perimeter = _____

Area = _____

Tile a Rectangle

Cut out the 1-inch unit squares along the dashed lines.
Try to cut as carefully and as straight as you can.

Perimeter and Area

Name _____

Tile a Rectangle

13 Use the 1-inch unit squares from page 311A
to cover the rectangle below.

Be sure there are no gaps between the unit squares.

Be sure no unit squares overlap.

14 Draw lines with a straight edge to show the unit
squares. The number of unit squares is the area
in square inches. What is the area?

_____

15 Use an inch ruler to measure the side lengths
of the rectangle. Label the length and the width.

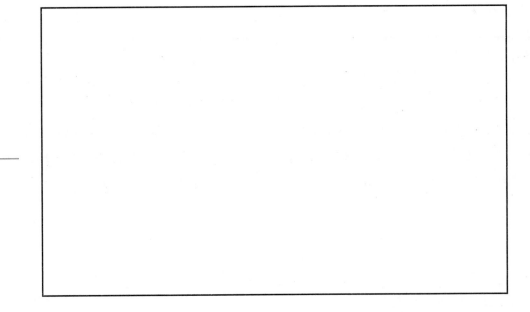

16 Write a multiplication equation to show the area.

_____

Tile a Rectangle (continued)

**Cover each rectangle with 1-inch unit squares.
Count the squares to find the area. Then write
an equation to show the area.**

17

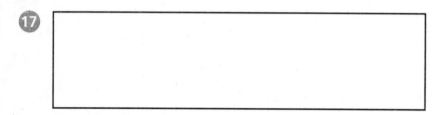

The area is _____. The equation is _____.

18

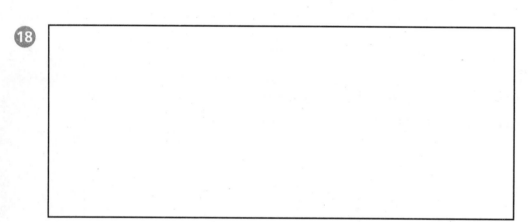

The area is _____. The equation is _____.

19 How many 1-inch unit squares
are needed to cover a rectangle
that is 7 inches long and
4 inches wide?

_____

20 What is the area of a rectangle
that is 7 inches long and
4 inches wide?

_____

✓ **Check Understanding**

Complete the sentences.

Perimeter measures _____.

Area measures _____.

Perimeter and Area

Write Different Equations for Area

1 Use the drawings. Show two ways to find the area of a rectangle that is 10 units long and 6 units wide.

2 Write equations for your two rectangle drawings.

_____   _____

3 Suppose the rectangle is 10 feet long and 6 feet wide. What is its area?

_____

4 Suppose the rectangle is 10 meters long and 6 meters wide. What is its area?

_____

5 Use drawings and write equations to show two ways to find the area of a rectangle that is 9 yards long and 5 yards wide.

_____   _____

CC SS Content Standards **3.MD.C.7, 3.MD.C.7.b, 3.MD.C.7.c, 3.MD.C.7.d, 3.MD.D.8** Mathematical Practices **MP1, MP2, MP4**

Side Lengths with Area and Perimeter **313**

Rectangle Equations and Drawings

Write an equation for each rectangle.

6

```
      3  +    5
   ┌──────┬──────────┐
 4 │      │          │
   └──────┴──────────┘
```

7

```
      2  +      4
   ┌──────┬──────────┐
 5 │      │          │
   │      │          │
   └──────┴──────────┘
```

8

```
     3  +      6
   ┌─────┬──────────┐
 3 │     │          │
   └─────┴──────────┘
```

9

```
      4   +   4
   ┌──────┬──────────┐
 4 │      │          │
   │      │          │
   └──────┴──────────┘
```

Draw a rectangle for each equation.

10 $(3 \times 3) + (3 \times 5) = 3 \times 8$

11 $(4 \times 5) + (4 \times 3) = 4 \times 8$

12 $(5 \times 3) + (5 \times 6) = 5 \times 9$

13 $(4 \times 6) + (4 \times 4) = 4 \times 10$

Side Lengths with Area and Perimeter

Find Unknown Side Lengths

Find the unknown side length in each rectangle.

14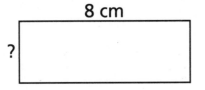

8 cm

?

Area = 72 sq cm

_____

15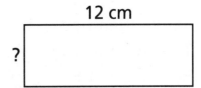

12 cm

?

Perimeter = 38 cm

_____

16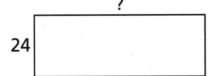

?

24

Perimeter = 64 cm

_____

17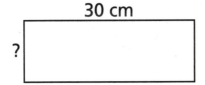

7 cm

?

Area = 56 sq cm

_____

18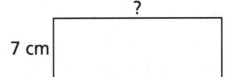

30 cm

?

Perimeter = 72 cm

_____

19

?

7 cm

Area = 63 sq cm

_____

20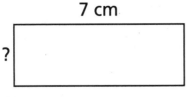

7 cm

?

Area = 28 sq cm

_____

21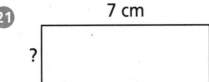

7 cm

?

Perimeter = 28 cm

_____

Unknown Side Length Problems

Solve. Draw a rectangle to represent the situation.   *Show your work.*

22 Alexander and his grandfather are tiling their rectangular kitchen floor. They need to use 42 tiles. They are making rows of 7 tiles. How many rows do they make?

_____

23 Martha has 63 quilt squares ready to sew together. She wants the quilt to be 9 rows long. How many squares will be in each row?

_____

24 Rick is painting a mural of different sizes of rectangles, with no gaps or overlaps of the rectangles. He has enough paint to cover 15 square yards. He wants the mural to be 3 yards long. How wide can the mural be?

_____

25 Mr. Baker is making a box using all of a 48-inch strip of oak. The box will be 14 inches wide. How long will the box be?

_____

✓**Check Understanding**
Draw and label a rectangle with an area of 36 square centimeters and one side length of 4 centimeters. Find the unknown side length. Then find the perimeter.

Name _____

Compare Rectangles with the Same Perimeter

Complete.

1 On a centimeter dot grid, draw all possible rectangles with a perimeter of 12 cm and sides whose lengths are whole centimeters. Label the lengths of two adjacent sides of each rectangle.

2 Find and label the area of each rectangle. In the table, record the lengths of the adjacent sides and the area of each rectangle.

3 Compare the shapes of the rectangles with the least area and greatest area.

Rectangles with Perimeter 12 cm	
Lengths of Two Adjacent Sides	Area

_____

_____

4 On a centimeter dot grid, draw all possible rectangles with a perimeter of 22 cm and sides whose lengths are whole centimeters. Label the lengths of two adjacent sides of each rectangle.

5 Find and label the area of each rectangle. In the table, record the lengths of the adjacent sides and the area of each rectangle.

Rectangles with Perimeter 22 cm	
Lengths of Two Adjacent Sides	Area

6 Compare the shapes of the rectangles with the least area and greatest area.

_____

_____

Compare Rectangles with the Same Area

7 On a centimeter dot grid, draw all possible rectangles with an area of 12 sq cm and sides whose lengths are whole centimeters. Label the lengths of two adjacent sides of each rectangle.

Rectangles with Area 12 sq cm	
Lengths of Two Adjacent Sides	Perimeter

8 Find and label the perimeter of each rectangle. In the table, record the lengths of the adjacent sides and the perimeter of each rectangle.

9 On a centimeter dot grid, draw all possible rectangles with an area of 18 sq cm and sides whose lengths are whole centimeters. Label the lengths of two adjacent sides of each rectangle.

Rectangles with Area 18 sq cm	
Lengths of Two Adjacent Sides	Perimeter

10 Find and label the perimeter of each rectangle. In the table, record the lengths of the adjacent sides and the perimeter of each rectangle.

11 Compare the shapes of the rectangles with the least and greatest perimeter.

_____

_____

_____

✓ **Check Understanding**

Draw and label a rectangle with the greatest area possible for a perimeter of 18 inches. The sides must be whole inches.

© Houghton Mifflin Harcourt Publishing Company

Compare Areas and Perimeters

Find Area by Decomposing into Rectangles

Decompose each figure into rectangles.
Then find the area of the figure.

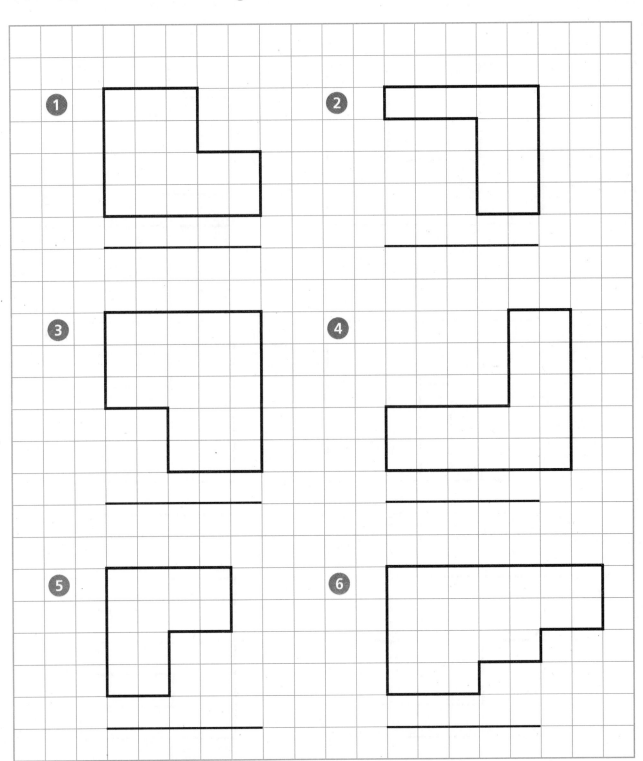

Find Area by Decomposing into Rectangles (continued)

**Decompose each figure into rectangles.
Then find the area of the figure.**

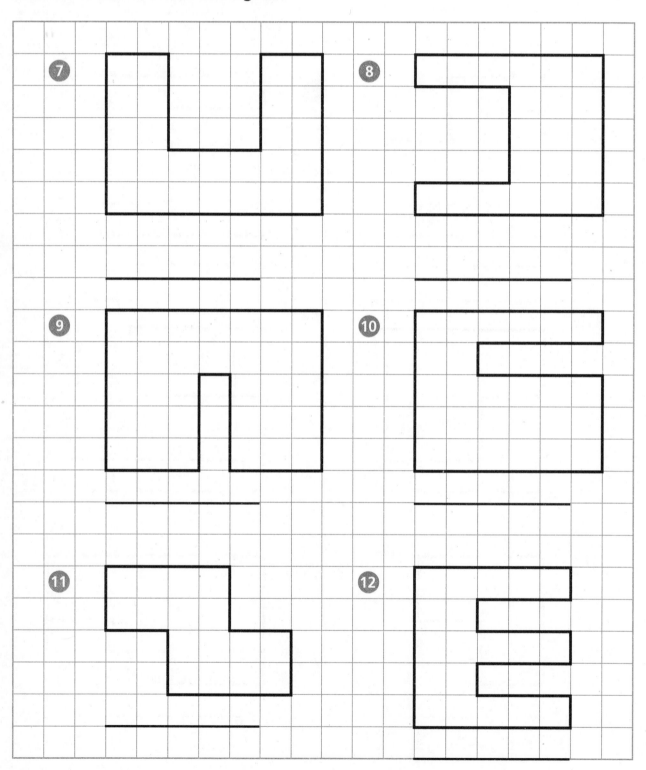

Area of Rectilinear Figures

Name _____

Find Area by Decomposing into Rectangles (continued)

**Decompose each figure into rectangles.
Then find the area of the figure.**

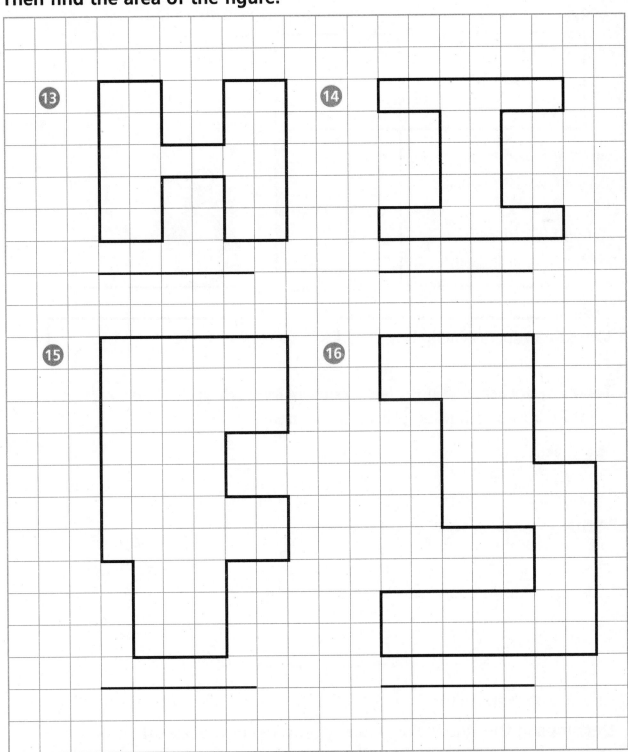

What's the Error?

Dear Math Students,

Today my teacher asked me to find the area of a figure. I knew that I could decompose the figure into rectangles. This is what I did.

Area of Rectangle 1:
3 x 6 = 18 square units

Area of Rectangle 2:
5 x 4 = 20 square units

Area of Figure:
18 + 20 = 38 square units

Is my work correct? If not, please correct my work and tell me what I did wrong. How do you know my answer is wrong?

Your friend,
Puzzled Penguin

17 Write an answer to Puzzled Penguin.

_____

_____

_____

_____

✓ **Check Understanding**

Decompose the figure Puzzled Penguin decomposed into rectangles a different way and find the area of the figure.

Area of Rectilinear Figures

Name _____

Solve Perimeter and Area Problems

Solve. Circle whether you need to find a perimeter, an area, or an unknown side length. Draw a figure to represent each situation.

Show your work.

1 The dimensions of a rectangular picture frame are 9 inches and 6 inches. What is the greatest size picture that would fit in the frame?

Perimeter   Area   Side Length

_____

2 A garden has the shape of a hexagon. Each side of the garden is 5 feet long. How much fence is needed to go around the garden?

Perimeter   Area   Side Length

_____

3 The length of a water slide is 9 yards. The slide is 2 yards wide. How much of the surface of the slide must be covered with water?

Perimeter   Area   Side Length

_____

4 Mr. Schmidt is installing 32 cubbies in the hallway. He puts 8 cubbies in each row. How many rows of cubbies can he make?

Perimeter   Area   Side Length

_____

Solve Perimeter and Area Problems (continued)

Solve. Circle whether you need to find a perimeter, an area, or an unknown side length. Draw a figure to represent each situation.

Show your work.

5 The floor of a delivery van has an area of 56 square feet and is 8 feet long. How many rows of 8 boxes that measure 1 foot by 1 foot can be put on the floor of the delivery van?

Perimeter   Area   Side Length

6 Zack is planning to make a flower garden. He has 24 one-yard sections of fence that he plans to place around the garden. He wants the garden to be as long as possible. What is the longest length he can use for the garden? How wide will the garden be?

Perimeter   Area   Side Length

7 An exercise room is 9 yards long and 7 yards wide. A locker room 8 yards long and 6 yards wide is attached to one end of the exercise room. How much floor space do the exercise room and the locker room take up?

Perimeter   Area   Side Length

8 Rosa's dog Sparky is 24 inches long. One side of Sparky's doghouse is 36 inches long and the other side is twice as long as Sparky. What is the distance around Sparky's doghouse?

Perimeter   Area   Side Length

Solve Perimeter and Area Problems

Solve Perimeter and Area Problems (continued)

Solve. Circle whether you need to find a perimeter, an area, or an unknown side length. Draw a figure to represent each situation.

Show your work.

9 Joanne made 16 fruit bars in a square pan. The fruit bars are 2 inches by 2 inches. What are the dimensions of the pan she used to bake the fruit bars?

Perimeter   Area   Side Length

10 A scout troop is making triangular pennants for their tents. Two sides of each pennant are 2 feet long and the third side is 1 foot long. How much binding tape is needed to go around 4 pennants?

Perimeter   Area   Side Length

11 A rectangular quilt is 5 feet wide and 7 feet long. How many feet of lace are needed to cover the edges of the quilt?

Perimeter   Area   Side Length

12 Amy has a piece of fleece fabric that is 4 feet wide and 6 feet long. How many squares of fleece fabric that are 1 foot wide and 1 foot long can she cut from the fabric?

Perimeter   Area   Side Length

Solve Perimeter and Area Problems (continued)

Solve. Circle whether you need to find a perimeter, an area, or an unknown side length. Draw a figure to represent each situation.

Show your work.

13 Vanita has 23 tiles with dimensions of 1 foot by 1 foot. She wants to tile a hallway that is 8 feet long and 3 feet wide. Does she have enough tiles? If not, how many more does she need?

Perimeter   Area   Side Length

_____

14 Mrs. Lee has 48 one-foot pieces of garden fence. What dimensions should she use for the garden to have as much room as possible?

Perimeter   Area   Side Length

_____

15 Martha has 27 striped squares and 27 dotted squares. She wants a quilt with rows of 6 squares. How many rows will the quilt have?

Perimeter   Area   Side Length

_____

16 A 20-mile bike path is in the shape of a triangle. Don rode 6 miles and 8 miles on the two sides. How long is the third side of the path?

Perimeter   Area   Side Length

_____

✓**Check Understanding**

Describe a real world situation when you would need to find perimeter and another for area.

© Houghton Mifflin Harcourt Publishing Company

Name _____

Explore Tangrams

Cut one tangram figure into pieces along the dotted lines. Try to cut as carefully and as straight as you can. Save the other figures to use later.

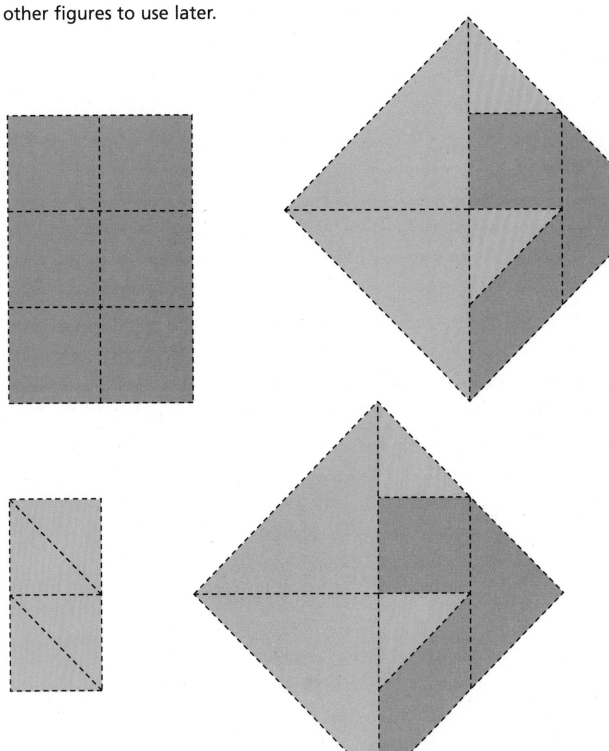

Tangram Shapes and Area **327A**

Explore Tangrams (continued)

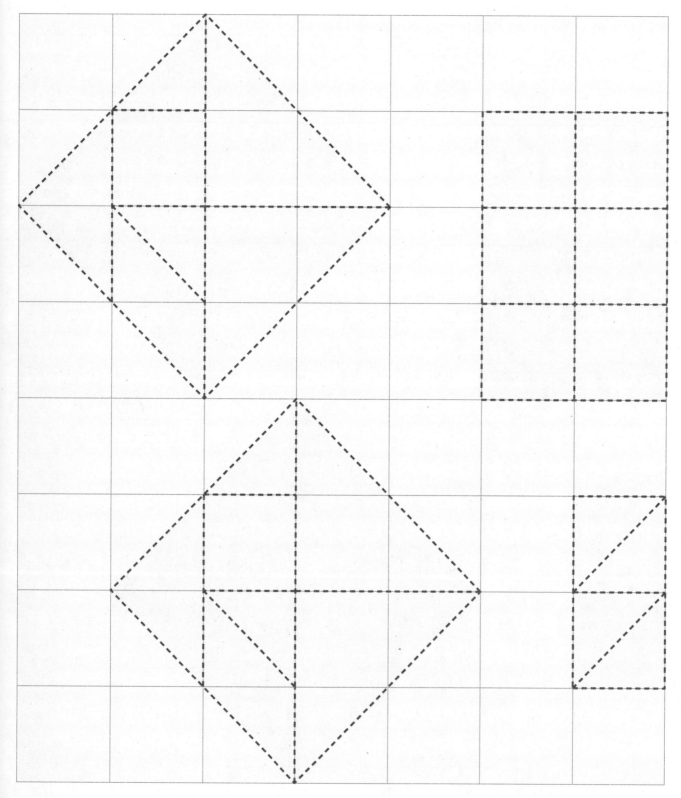

Tangram Shapes and Area

Name

Solve Tangram Puzzles

Use the tangram pieces from page 327A.

1 Make this bird. When you finish, draw lines to show how you placed the pieces.

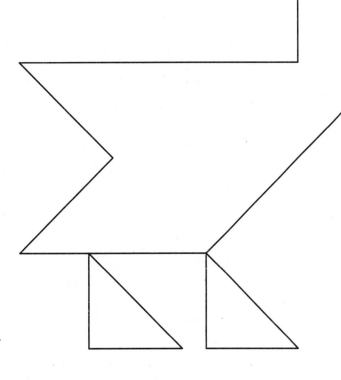

2 Make this rectangle. Draw lines to show how you placed the pieces. Hint: You do not need all the pieces.

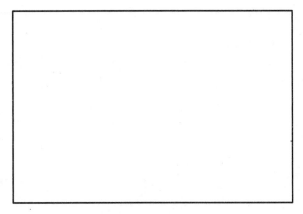

Content Standards **3.MD.C.6**
Mathematical Practices **MP7**

Solve Tangram Puzzles (continued)

Use the tangram pieces. Draw lines to show how you placed the pieces.

3 Make this boat.

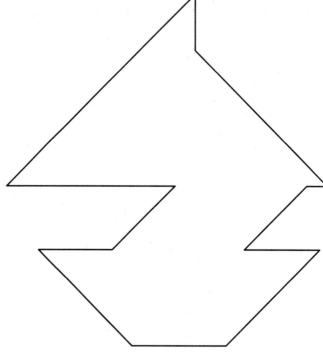

4 Make this tree.

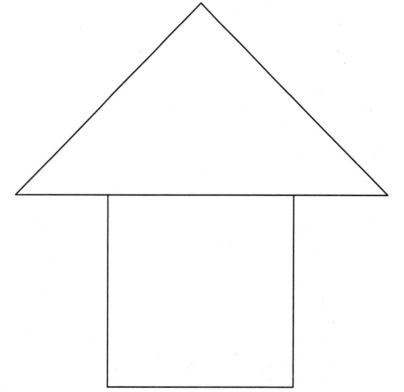

Tangram Shapes and Area

Use Tangram Pieces to Find Area

5 Use all seven tangram pieces. Cover this rectangle.

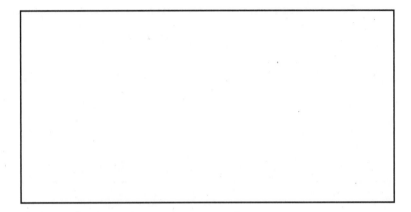

6 What is the area of the rectangle?

_____

7 Use any tangram pieces. Cover this rectangle.

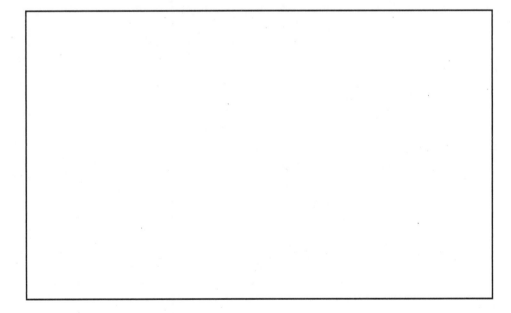

8 What is the area of the rectangle?

_____

Use Tangram Pieces to Find Area (continued)

Use any tangram pieces. Cover each rectangle.

9
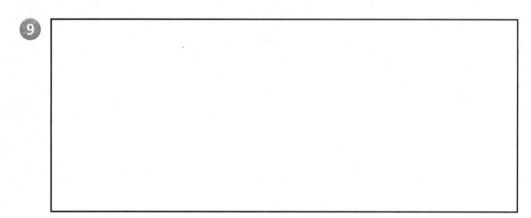

What is the area of the rectangle?

_____

10

What is the area of the square?

_____

Tangram Shapes and Area

Use Tangram Pieces to Find Area (continued)

Use any tangram pieces. Cover each figure.

What is the area of the square?

_____

What is the area of the rectangle?

_____

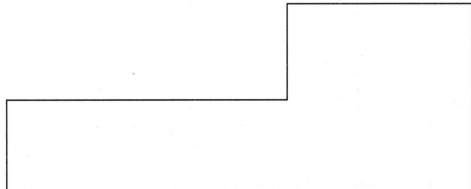

What is the area of the figure?

Use Tangram Pieces to Find Area (continued)

Use any tangram pieces. Cover each figure.

14 What is the area of the triangle?

_____

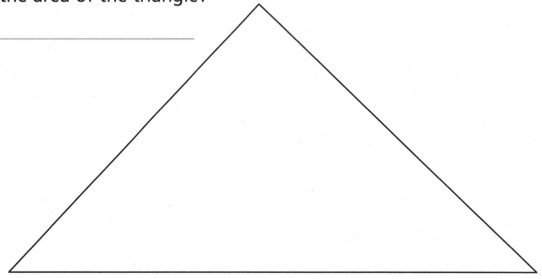

15

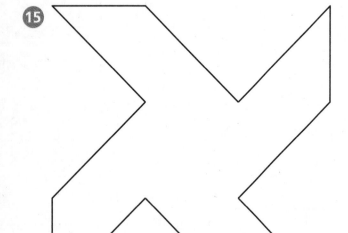

What is the area of the figure?

_____

✓ **Check Understanding**

What is the area of a figure made with the seven

tangram pieces? _____

Write the correct answer.

Show your work.

1 What is the area of the figure?

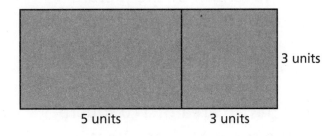

5 units   3 units

3 units

_____

2 The area of a rectangle is 80 square units. The length of one of the shorter sides is 8 units. What is the length of one of the longer sides?

_____

3 Rectangles *A* and *B* have the same areas. Rectangle *A* is 3 inches wide and 8 inches long. If Rectangle *B* is 4 inches wide, how long is it?

_____

Use the centimeter dot grid for Exercises 4–5.

4 Which figure has an area of 18 square centimeters?

_____

5 What is the perimeter of each figure?

_____

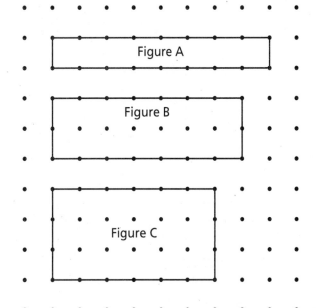

Figure A

Figure B

Figure C

Solve.

1 Marcy uses 48 inches of ribbon to frame a rectangular picture. The length of the picture is 14 inches. How wide is the picture?

_____

2 A rectangular carpet has an area of 110 square feet. The length of the rug is 11 feet. What is the width of the rug?

_____

3 On the centimeter grid below, draw two different rectangles with a perimeter of 12 centimeters. Label the area of each figure.

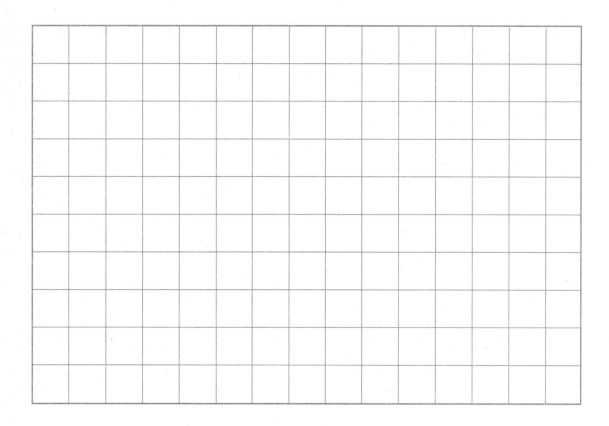

Make Fraction Strips

Fraction Strips **335A**

Fraction Strips

Name _____

Halves, Fourths, and Eighths

VOCABULARY
equivalent fractions

Two fractions are **equivalent fractions** if they name the same part of a whole.

Use your halves, fourths, and eighths strips to complete Exercises 1–4.

$\frac{1}{2}$				$\frac{1}{2}$			
$\frac{1}{4}$		$\frac{1}{4}$		$\frac{1}{4}$		$\frac{1}{4}$	
$\frac{1}{8}$	$\frac{1}{8}$	$\frac{1}{8}$	$\frac{1}{8}$	$\frac{1}{8}$	$\frac{1}{8}$	$\frac{1}{8}$	$\frac{1}{8}$

1 If you compare your halves strip and your fourths strip, you can see that 2 fourths are the same as 1 half.

Complete these two equations:

_____ fourths = 1 half $\dfrac{\boxed{}}{4} = \dfrac{1}{2}$

2 How many eighths are in one half? _____

Complete these two equations:

_____ eighths = 1 half $\dfrac{\boxed{}}{8} = \dfrac{1}{2}$

3 What are two fractions that are equivalent to $\frac{1}{2}$?

_____

4 How many eighths are in one fourth? _____

Complete these two equations:

_____ eighths = 1 fourth $\dfrac{\boxed{}}{8} = \dfrac{1}{4}$

Thirds and Sixths

Use your thirds and sixths strips to answer Exercises 5–6.

5 How many sixths are in one third? _____

Complete these two equations:

_____ sixths = 1 third $\frac{\square}{6} = \frac{1}{3}$

6 How many sixths are in two thirds? _____

Complete these two equations:

_____ sixths = 2 thirds $\frac{\square}{6} = \frac{2}{3}$

What's the Error?

Dear Math Students,

Today my teacher asked me to name a fraction that is equivalent to $\frac{1}{2}$.

I wrote $\frac{2}{6} = \frac{1}{2}$.

Is my answer correct? If not, please correct my work and tell me what I did wrong.

Your Friend,
Puzzled Penguin

7 Write an answer to Puzzled Penguin.

_____

_____

_____

✓ Check Understanding

Name another fraction equivalent to $\frac{1}{2}$ that Puzzled Penguin could have written. _____

Introduce Equivalence

Name _____

Equivalent Fractions on Number Lines

1 Complete each number line. Show all fractions including each fraction for 1.

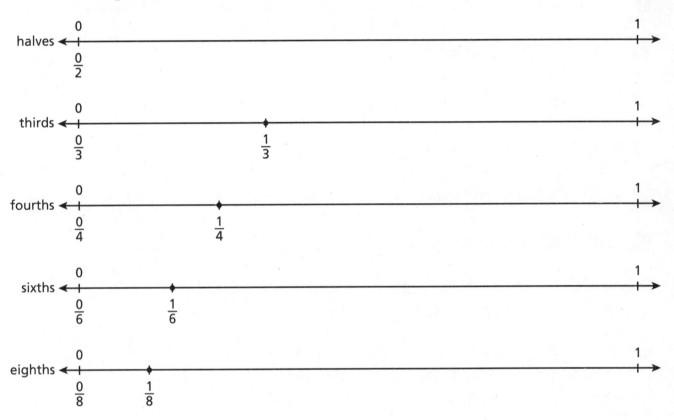

halves
$\frac{0}{2}$

thirds
$\frac{0}{3}$ $\frac{1}{3}$

fourths
$\frac{0}{4}$ $\frac{1}{4}$

sixths
$\frac{0}{6}$ $\frac{1}{6}$

eighths
$\frac{0}{8}$ $\frac{1}{8}$

2 Write an equivalence chain with fractions that equal $\frac{2}{2}$.

_____

3 Why are the fractions in the equivalence chain for $\frac{2}{2}$ equal?

_____

4 Why does the length of unit fractions grow smaller as their denominators get larger?

_____

_____

© Houghton Mifflin Harcourt Publishing Company

Content Standards 3.NF.A.2.a, 3.NF.A.2.b, 3.NF.A.3, 3.NF.A.3.a, 3.NF.A.3.b, 3.NF.A.3.c
Mathematical Practices MP1, MP2

Equivalent Fractions **337**

Equivalence Chains

Use your number lines from page 337 to write an equivalence chain.

5 With fractions that equal $\frac{1}{2}$ _____

6 With fractions that equal $\frac{1}{3}$ _____

7 With fractions that equal $\frac{2}{3}$ _____

8 With fractions that equal $\frac{1}{4}$ _____

9 With fractions that equal $\frac{3}{4}$ _____

10 With fractions that equal $\frac{8}{8}$ _____

Solve. Use what you have learned about equivalent fractions and about comparing fractions.

Show your work.

11 Jaime has $\frac{1}{2}$ foot of red ribbon and $\frac{4}{8}$ foot of green ribbon. Does he have more red ribbon or green ribbon?

_____

12 Chin and Maya collected conch shells at the beach. They both used the same kind of basket. Chin's basket is $\frac{3}{4}$ filled, and Maya's basket is $\frac{3}{3}$ filled. Who collected more shells?

_____

✓**Check Understanding**

Explain how you could use a number line to help you solve Problem 12.

Equivalent Fractions

Solve Fraction Problems

Solve. Draw diagrams or number lines if you need to.

1 The shelves in Roger's bookcase are $\frac{7}{8}$ yard long. Ana's bookcase has shelves that are $\frac{5}{8}$ yard long. Whose bookcase has longer shelves? How do you know?

2 Rosa buys $\frac{3}{4}$ pound of cheese. Lucy buys $\frac{3}{8}$ pound of cheese. Who buys more cheese? Explain your answer.

3 Vera has same-size muffin pans. She fills $\frac{8}{4}$ pans with cranberry muffins and $\frac{8}{6}$ pans with banana muffins. Does Vera have fewer cranberry muffins or banana muffins? How do you know?

4 Lester walks $\frac{3}{4}$ mile to school. Bert said that he walks farther because he walks $\frac{6}{8}$ mile to school. Is his statement correct? Explain your answer.

5 Rusty painted $\frac{5}{6}$ of a mural for a hallway. Has he painted more than half of the mural? Explain your answer. *Hint*: Find an equivalent fraction in sixths for $\frac{1}{2}$.

Solve Fraction Problems (continued)

Solve. Draw diagrams or number lines if you need to.

6 Pearl used $\frac{3}{3}$ yard of fabric to make a pillow. Julia made her pillow from $\frac{4}{4}$ yard of fabric. They both paid $5 a yard for their fabric. Who paid more for fabric? How do you know?

_____

_____

7 Deena's pan has a total of $\frac{2}{5}$ liter of water. John's pan has a total of $\frac{5}{2}$ liters of water. Whose pan has more water? How do you know?

_____

_____

8 Andy, Lu, and Carlos have $\frac{3}{3}$, $\frac{3}{4}$, and $\frac{3}{6}$ dozen pencils, but not in that order. Andy has the fewest pencils and Lu has the most. How many pencils does each boy have? Explain.

_____

_____

✓ **Check Understanding**

Draw fraction bars or a number line to compare the fractions in Problem 8.

© Houghton Mifflin Harcourt Publishing Company

Problem Solving with Fractions

Fractions and Paper Folding

The art of paper folding began in China. Later, Japan's version of paper folding, called origami, became very popular. Origami sculptures are made by folding and sculpting a flat sheet of square paper without cuts or glue.

Complete.

1 Fold a square sheet of paper in half diagonally. What part of the square is each triangle?

_____

2 Fold the paper in half again. What part of the square is each triangle?

_____

3 Fold the paper in half again. Open the paper. What part of the square is each triangle?

_____

4 Explain how you know the eight parts have the same area.

_____

_____

5 Fold four triangles to the center as shown on the right. What part of the square is each triangle? Explain how you know.

_____

_____

_____

This basic origami fold is used for making many objects.

CC SS Content Standards **3.NF.A.1, 3.NF.A.3, 3.NF.A.3.a, 3.NF.A.3.b, 3.G.A.2** Mathematical Practices **MP2, MP7**

Fractions and Design

Complete.

6 Fold a square sheet of paper in half three times.
Open the paper. Choose two different colors.
Color every other rectangle or triangle one color.
Color the other rectangles or triangles the second color.

7 Write 3 equivalent fractions for the part of the square
that has the same color.

_____

8 Predict the number of shapes you would make
if you folded the square 4 times. Explain.

_____

_____

_____

_____

Focus on Mathematical Practices

Name _____

Date _____

Complete.

1 How many sixths are in one third? _____

Complete these two equations:

_____ sixths = 1 third

$$\frac{\square}{6} = \frac{1}{3}$$

2 How many eighths are in one half? _____

Complete these two equations:

_____ eighths = 1 half

$$\frac{\square}{8} = \frac{1}{2}$$

3 Write an equivalence chain with three fractions that equal $\frac{1}{4}$.

_____

Complete the number line. Show the fraction for 1.

4
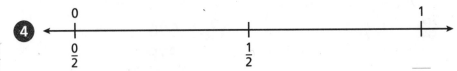

Solve.   *Show your work.*

5 Monica buys $\frac{2}{3}$ pound of apples. Nicole buys $\frac{5}{6}$ pound of peaches. Do the apples or the peaches weigh more? Explain your answer.

_____

_____

Name _____ **Date** _____

Multiply or divide.

1 $7 \times 0 = \boxed{}$

2 $12 \div 2 = \boxed{}$

3 $8 \times 3 = \boxed{}$

4 $16 \div 4 = \boxed{}$

5 $3 \times 7 = \boxed{}$

6 $42 \div 6 = \boxed{}$

7 $6 \times 8 = \boxed{}$

8 $81 \div 9 = \boxed{}$

9 $8 \times 7 = \boxed{}$

Add or subtract.

10
$$\begin{array}{r} 885 \\ -\ 345 \\ \hline \end{array}$$

11
$$\begin{array}{r} 326 \\ +\ 421 \\ \hline \end{array}$$

12
$$\begin{array}{r} 508 \\ -\ 329 \\ \hline \end{array}$$

13
$$\begin{array}{r} 264 \\ +\ 338 \\ \hline \end{array}$$

14
$$\begin{array}{r} 623 \\ -\ 365 \\ \hline \end{array}$$

15
$$\begin{array}{r} 478 \\ +\ 385 \\ \hline \end{array}$$

1 A park ranger has 32 feet of fencing to fence four sides
of a rectangular recycling site. What is the greatest area
of recycling site that the ranger can fence? Explain how
you know.

2 Use the fractions to label each point on
the number line.

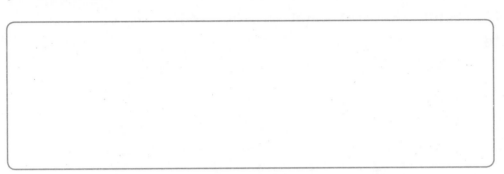

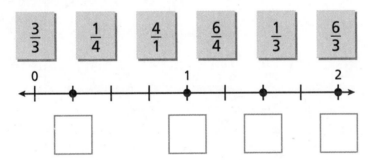

3 Select the fraction that would be included in an
equivalence chain for $\frac{6}{6}$. Mark all that apply.

Ⓐ $\frac{3}{3}$ Ⓓ $\frac{5}{5}$

Ⓑ $\frac{3}{6}$ Ⓔ $\frac{6}{1}$

Ⓒ $\frac{4}{4}$

4 Steve makes a banner with an area of 8 square feet. On the grid, draw all possible rectangles with an area of 8 square feet and sides whose lengths are whole feet. Label the lengths of two adjacent sides of each rectangle. Label each rectangle with its perimeter.

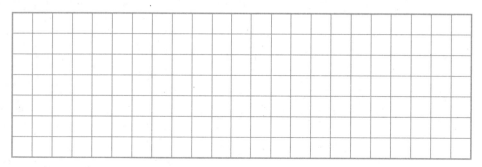

Compare the perimeters of the banners. What do you notice about their shapes?

5 Draw a line from the fraction on the left to match the equivalent fraction or number on the right.

$\frac{4}{6}$ •   • 8

$\frac{8}{1}$ •   • $\frac{2}{3}$

$\frac{3}{4}$ •   • 1

$\frac{2}{8}$ •   • $\frac{6}{8}$

$\frac{2}{2}$ •   • $\frac{1}{4}$

6 Mark the number line to show the fractions. First
divide the number line into correct unit fractions.

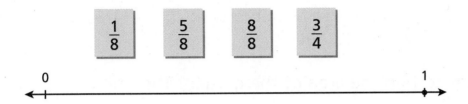

7 Hailey's patio is 9 feet long. If the area of the patio is
90 square feet, how wide is the patio?

_____ feet

8 Mr. Gomez hangs a mural on the classroom wall. Find the
perimeter and area of the mural.

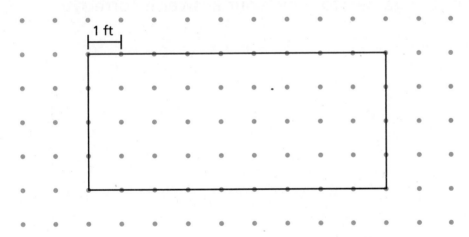

Perimeter: _____ feet

Area: _____ square feet

Name ______________________ Date ______________________

9 Liana plants a vegetable garden in two sections. She plants corn in a section that is 5 meters long and 6 meters wide. She plants squash in a section that is 3 meters long and 6 meters wide.

Part A

Describe one way to find the area of the garden. Then find the area.

Area: ____________ square meters

Part B

Draw a picture of the garden to show your answer is correct.

10 Dan walks $\frac{5}{8}$ mile to school. Beth walks $\frac{3}{4}$ mile to school.

Part A

Who walks farther? Label and shade the circles to help solve the problem.

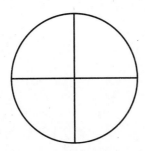 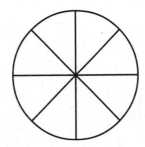

_____ walks farther.

Part B

Suppose Dan walks $\frac{6}{8}$ mile instead of $\frac{5}{8}$ mile. Who walks farther? How do the circles help you decide?

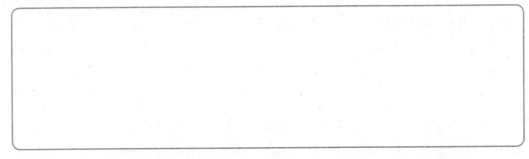

11 Henry and Reiko both use 1 yard of ribbon to make bows. Write two different fractions to show that Henry and Reiko use the same amount of ribbon.

Henry uses _____ yard.

Reiko uses _____ yard.

12 Draw a line from the figure to the area of the figure.

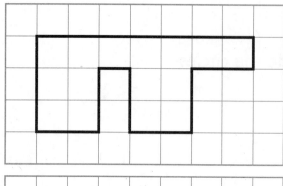

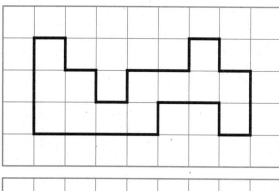

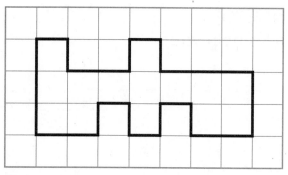

• 13 square units

• 14 square units

• 15 square units

13 Riki cuts two decagons out of cardboard. Then he glues yarn around the edges. How much yarn does Riki use if each edge of the decagon is 8 centimeters?

_____ centimeters

14 Rino needs $\frac{1}{2}$ cup of pineapple juice for a shake. What are two other fractions equivalent to $\frac{1}{2}$?

_____

Dog Park

The town of Springfield is planning to create a rectangular dog park. The park will be 8 yards long and 10 yards wide.

1 How much fencing is needed to go around the park?

_____

2 What is the area of the planned park?

_____

3 Half of the park will have a lawn and one fourth of the park will be covered with gravel. Shade the model below to show the lawn and the part with gravel.

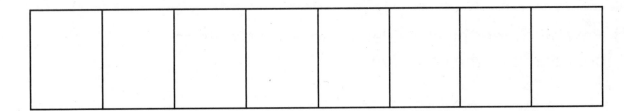

4 The remaining area of the park will have benches. What fraction of the total area will have benches?

_____

5 Write two equivalent fractions to represent the area of the park with the lawn.

_____

The town of Springfield plans to make the dog park larger.

5. The town will add 20 square yards of land next to the original park. Draw and label the possible dimensions of the addition.

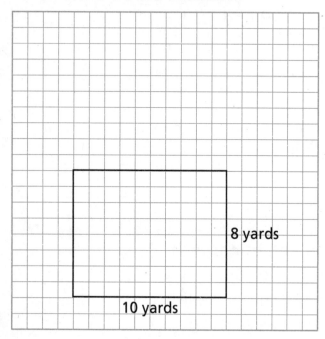

8 yards

10 yards

6. How much fencing is needed to go around outside boundaries of the new park?

_____

7. Use the grid below to design your own dog park. Each square represents 1 square unit. The area of your park must be 24 square units. Label the drawing with the perimeter of the park.

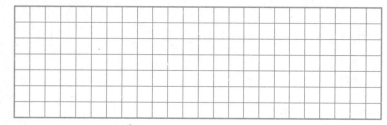

Dear Family:

In this unit, your child will solve addition, subtraction, multiplication, and division problems involving unknown addends and factors.

- If one of the addends is unknown, it can be found by subtracting the known addend from the total or by counting on from the known addend to the total.

- If the total is unknown, it can be found by adding the addends.

- If one of the factors is unknown, it can be found by dividing the product by the other factor.

- If the product is unknown, it can be found by multiplying the factors.

Math Mountains are used to show a total and two addends. Students can use the Math Mountain to write an equation and then solve the equation to find the unknown.

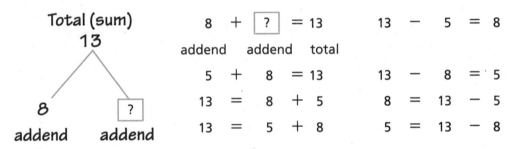

Equations with numbers alone on the left are also emphasized to help with the understanding of algebra.

Comparison Bars are used to solve problems that involve one amount that is more than or less than another amount. Drawing Comparison Bars can help a student organize the information in the problem in order to find the unknown smaller amount, the unknown larger amount, or the difference.

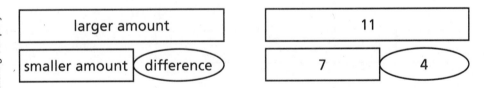

Please contact me if you have any questions or comments.

Sincerely,
Your child's teacher

CC SS Unit 6 addresses the following standards from the Common Core State Standards for Mathematics: **3.OA.A.3, 3.OA.A.4, 3.OA.D.8, 3.NBT.A.2,** and for all Mathematical Practices.

Estimada familia:

En esta unidad, su niño resolverá sumas, restas, multiplicaciones y divisiones con sumandos o factores desconocidos.

- Si uno de los sumandos se desconoce, puede hallarse restando el sumando conocido del total, o contando hacia adelante desde el sumando conocido hasta llegar al total.

- Si el total se desconoce, puede hallarse sumando los sumandos.

- Si uno de los factores se desconoce, puede hallarse dividiendo el producto entre el otro factor.

- Si el producto se desconoce, puede hallarse multiplicando los factores.

Para mostrar un total y dos sumandos se usan las **Montañas matemáticas**. Los estudiantes puede usarlas para escribir una ecuación, y al resolverla, hallar el elemento desconocido.

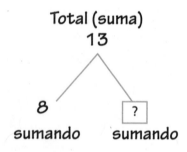

$$8 + \boxed{?} = 13 \qquad 13 - 5 = 8$$

sumando sumando total

$$5 + 8 = 13 \qquad 13 - 8 = 5$$
$$13 = 8 + 5 \qquad 8 = 13 - 5$$
$$13 = 5 + 8 \qquad 5 = 13 - 8$$

Se hace énfasis en las ecuaciones que tienen números solos en el lado izquierdo, para facilitar la comprensión del álgebra.

Para resolver problemas con una cantidad que es más o menos que otra, se usan **Barras de comparación**. Estas barras sirven para organizar la información del problema, y hallar así, la cantidad desconocida más pequeña, la más grande o la diferencia.

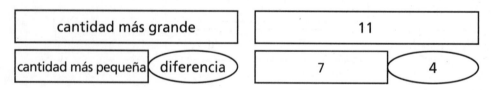

Si tiene alguna pregunta o algún comentario, por favor comuníquese conmigo.

Atentamente,
El maestro de su niño

© Houghton Mifflin Harcourt Publishing Company

CC SS En la Unidad 6 se aplican los siguientes estándares de los Estándares estatales comunes de matemáticas: **3.0A.A.3,** **3.0A.A.4, 3.0A.D.8, 3.NBT.A.2,** y todos los de Prácticas matemáticas.

addend

sum

total

One of two or more numbers
to be added together to find
a sum.

Example:

$$8 + 4 = 12$$

addend   addend   sum

The answer when adding
two or more addends.

Example:

$$37 + 52 = 89$$

addend   addend   sum

The answer when adding
two or more addends.
The sum of two or more
numbers.

Example:

$$672 + 228 = 900$$

addend   *addend*   total
sum

Name _____

Math Mountains and Equations

VOCABULARY
total
addend
sum

Complete.

1 Look at the Math Mountain and the 8 equations.
What relationships do you see? In each equation,
label each number as an **addend** (*A*) or the **total** (*T*).

sum
total
110

70   40
addend   addend

$110 = 70 + 40$ $70 + 40 = 110$

___ ___ ___   ___ ___ ___

$110 = 40 + 70$ $40 + 70 = 110$

___ ___ ___   ___ ___ ___

$40 = 110 - 70$ $110 - 70 = 40$

___ ___ ___   ___ ___ ___

$70 = 110 - 40$ $110 - 40 = 70$

___ ___ ___   ___ ___ ___

2 Write the 8 equations for this Math Mountain.
Label each number as the total (*T*) or an addend (*A*).

_____   _____

140

80   60

_____   _____

_____   _____

_____   _____

Solve and Discuss

Solve each problem. Label your answers.

Show your work.

3 **Add To** Chris's group picked 80 apples. His mother's group picked 60 more apples. How many apples do they have now?

_____

4 **Take From** Chris's group had 140 apples. They ate 80 of them. How many apples do they have now?

_____

5 **Put Together/Take Apart** Alison's class brought 70 juice boxes to the picnic. Taylor's class brought 50 juice boxes. How many juice boxes did they bring altogether?

_____

6 **Put Together/Take Apart** There are 120 juice boxes at the picnic. Alison puts 70 on tables and leaves the rest in the cooler. How many juice boxes are in the cooler?

_____

Addition and Subtraction Situations

Name _____

Represent Word Problems with Math Tools

The equations and Math Mountains below
show the word problems on page 356.

Add To

80   +   60   =   ☐

Chris's   Mom's   total
group   group

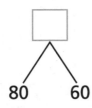

80   60

Take From

140   −   80   =   ☐

total   ate   now

140

80   ☐

Put Together/Take Apart

70   +   50   =   ☐

Alison's   Taylor's   total
class   class

☐

70   50

Put Together/Take Apart

120   −   70   =   ☐

total   tables   cooler

70   +   ☐   =   120

tables   cooler   total

120

70   ☐

7 Write the unknown numbers in the boxes.

8 How are these math tools the same? How are they different?

9 **Math Journal** Write a word problem for this

equation: 110 − 40 = ☐ . Then solve it.

PATH to FLUENCY Discuss the = and ≠ Signs

An expression is a combination of numbers, variables, and/or operation signs. Expressions do not have an equal sign.

An equation is made up of two equal quantities or expressions. An equal sign (=) is used to show that the two sides are equal.

$8 = 5 + 3$ $\qquad$ $4 + 2 = 6$ $\qquad$ $7 = 7$ $\qquad$ $3 + 2 = 2 + 3$

The "is not equal to" sign (≠) shows that two quantities are not equal.

$7 \neq 5 + 3$ $\qquad$ $4 + 2 \neq 8$ $\qquad$ $7 \neq 6$ $\qquad$ $5 + 2 \neq 1 + 1 + 3$

10 Use the = sign to write three equations. Vary how many numbers you have on each side of the sign.

_____

_____

_____

11 Use the ≠ sign to write three "is not equal to" statements. Vary how many numbers you have on each side of the sign.

_____

_____

_____

Write a number to make the number sentence true.

12 $160 = \boxed{} + 90$

13 $30 + \boxed{} \neq 120$

14 $150 - \boxed{} = 70$

15 $\boxed{} \neq 140 - 70$

Write = or ≠ to make a true number sentence.

16 $80 + 20 + 40 \bigcirc 90 + 50$

17 $80 \bigcirc 60 - 20$

✓Check Understanding

Draw a Math Mountain for this problem: Cory had 12 grapes. He ate 4 of them. How many grapes does he have now? Then write an equation for the problem and solve.

Solve Unknown Addend Word Problems

Draw a Math Mountain and write and label an equation with a variable. Then solve each problem.

Show your work.

1 **Put Together/Take Apart: Unknown Addend**
There were 90 girls and some boys in an after-school program. 160 children were in the program in all. How many boys were in the after-school program?

_____

2 **Put Together/Take Apart: Unknown Addend**
There were 150 people at the park. 70 were playing soccer. The others were playing softball. How many people were playing softball?

_____

3 **Add To: Unknown Addend** Jan planted 80 tulips last week. Today she planted some roses. Now she has 170 flowers. How many roses did she plant?

_____

4 **Take From: Unknown Addend** Tim's team had 140 tennis balls. Then his brother's team borrowed some. Now Tim's team has 60 tennis balls. How many did his brother's team borrow?

_____

CC SS Content Standards **3.NBT.A.2, 3.OA.A.3, 3.OA.A.4**
Mathematical Practices **MP1, MP2, MP4, MP5**

Represent Unknown Addends with Math Tools

The equations and Math Mountains below show
the word problems on page 359.

Put Together/Take Apart: Unknown Addend

$$90 \quad + \quad b \quad = \quad 160$$
girls   boys   children

children
160

90
girls   boys

Put Together/Take Apart: Unknown Addend

$$150 \quad - \quad s \quad = \quad 70$$
park   softball   soccer

park
150

70
softball   soccer

Add To: Unknown Addend

$$80 \quad + \quad r \quad = \quad 170$$
tulips   roses   flowers

flowers
170

80
tulips   roses

Take From: Unknown Addend

$$140 \quad - \quad b \quad = \quad 60$$
balls   some   now

tennis balls
140

60
some   now

5 Write the unknown numbers in the boxes and above the variables.

6 How are these math tools alike? How are they different?

Name _____

Solve Unknown Factor Word Problems

Write an equation for each word problem. Use a variable to represent the unknown factor. Then solve the problem.

Show your work.

7 A toymaker has 36 boxes of toy trains to ship to 4 toy shops. Each shop will get the same number of boxes. How many boxes of toy trains will each shop get?

_____

8 There are 56 cars in a parking lot. There are 8 rows and the same number of cars is in each row. How many cars are in each row?

_____

9 An apartment building has 42 apartments. There are 6 apartments on each floor. How many floors are in the apartment building?

_____

10 There are 48 students in the marching band. The students stand in equal rows of 8. How many rows of students are there?

_____

Word Problems with Unknown Addends or Unknown Factors **361**

Solve Unknown Factor Word Problems (continued)

**Write an equation for each word problem.
Use a variable to represent the unknown
factor. Then solve the problem.**

Show your work.

11 Daniel is setting up seats for the third
grade play. There are 6 seats in each row.
There are 54 seats in all. How many rows
of seats are there?

_____

12 Mrs. Martinez is sewing buttons on
4 costumes. Each costume has the same
number of buttons. There are 32 buttons
in all. How many buttons are on each costume?

_____

13 The library received 63 new books. The librarian
will put 7 books on each shelf of a bookcase.
How many shelves are there?

_____

14 There are 72 juice boxes for the class
picnic. The juice boxes are in packs of 8.
How many packs of juice boxes are there?

_____

Check Understanding
Draw a picture to represent Problem 14:
72 juice boxes in packs of 8.

Word Problems with Unknown Addends or Unknown Factors

Name _____

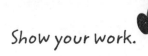

Solve Unknown Start Problems

Solve each problem. Label your answers.   *Show your work.*

1 Add To: Unknown Start Greta puts some beads on a string. Then she puts on 70 more beads. Now there are 130 beads on the string. How many beads did she put on the string to start?

_____

2 Take From: Unknown Start Greta puts some beads on a string. Then 70 of the beads fell off the string. There are 60 beads still on the string. How many beads were there at first?

_____

3 Add To: Unknown Start Patrick was carrying some booklets. His teacher asked him to carry 30 more booklets. Now he has 110 booklets. How many booklets did he start with?

_____

4 Take From: Unknown Start Patricia was carrying some pencils. Her friend took 30 of them. Patricia has 80 pencils left. How many pencils was she carrying at first?

_____

CC SS Content Standards **3.NBT.A.2, 3.OA.A.3, 3.OA.A.4**
Mathematical Practices **MP1, MP2, MP4, MP5**

Represent Unknown Start Problems with Math Tools

The equations and Math Mountains below show the word problems on page 363.

Add To: Unknown Start

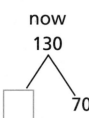

now
130

start   more

Situation Equation:

☐ + 70 = 130

start   more   now

solution equations:

70 + ☐ = 130

130 − 70 = ☐

Take From: Unknown Start

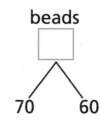

beads

70   60

fell   on
off

Situation Equation:

☐ − 70 = 60

beads   fell   on
         off

solution equation:

60 + 70 = ☐

Add To: Unknown Start

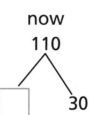

now
110

start   more

Situation Equation:

☐ + 30 = 110

start   more   now

Solution Equations:

30 + ☐ = 110

110 − 30 = ☐

Take From: Unknown Start

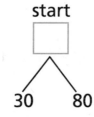

start

30   80

friend   now

Situation Equation:

☐ − 30 = 80

start   friend   now

Solution Equation:

80 + 30 = ☐

5 Write the unknown numbers in the boxes.

6 How are these math tools alike? How are they different?

_____

_____

Word Problems with Unknown Starts

Name _____

Write Situation and Solution Equations

**Write a situation equation and a solution equation.
Then solve the problem.**

7 Eight vans with the same number of students in each
van took 40 students to the science center for a field trip.
How many students were in each van?

Situation Equation: _____

Solution Equation: _____

8 Fiona made some barrettes. She put 9 beads on each
barrette. If she used 63 beads, how many barrettes did
she make?

Situation Equation: _____

Solution Equation: _____

9 A bird sanctuary has 81 birds. There are 9 birds in
each section. How many section are there?

Situation Equation: _____

Solution Equation: _____

10 Enrique has 56 miniature cars. He put the same
number of cars on 7 shelves in his room. How many
cars are on each shelf?

Situation Equation: _____

Solution Equation: _____

Write Situation and Solution Equations (continued)

**Write a situation equation and a solution equation.
Then solve the problem.**

11 A group of 48 students from 8 schools are competing
in the science fair. Each school sends the same
number of students. How many students are
competing from each school?

Situation Equation: _____

Solution Equation: _____

12 An array on one wall in an art gallery has
27 photographs. Each row has 9 photographs.
How many rows are there?

Situation Equation: _____

Solution Equation: _____

13 Jody bought 4 bags of lemons. The same number
of lemons was in each bag. There were a total of
36 lemons. How many lemons were in each bag?

Situation Equation: _____

Solution Equation: _____

14 A hardware store sold a number of furnace filters.
There were 6 filters in each box. If they sold
54 furnace filters, how many boxes of filters
did the hardware store sell?

Situation Equation: _____

Solution Equation: _____

✓ Check Understanding

Explain the difference between a situation
equation and a solution equation.

　　　　　　　Word Problems with Unknown Starts

Name _____

Compare Numbers

Compare the numbers. Write >, <, or = in each ◯.

1 34 ◯ 86

2 97 ◯ 67

3 653 ◯ 663

4 875 ◯ 587

5 752 ◯ 572

6 864 ◯ 846

7 1,932 ◯ 2,951

8 2,633 ◯ 2,487

9 3,478 ◯ 3,478

10 4,786 ◯ 4,876

Order Numbers

Write the numbers in order from greatest to least.

11 69; 20; 81

_____

12 381; 124; 197

_____

Write the numbers in order from least to greatest.

13 2,245; 1,642; 787

_____

14 1,987; 1,898; 1,789

_____

Discuss Comparison Problems

Solve each problem. Label your answers.

David has 5 marbles. Ana has 8 marbles.

15 How many more marbles
does Ana have than David? _____

16 How many fewer marbles
does David have than Ana? _____

Here are two ways to represent the comparison situation.

Comparison Drawing

Ana ○○○○○○○○
David ○○○○○

Comparison Bars

Ana	8

David	5	?

Claire has 8 marbles. Sasha has 15 marbles.

Show your work.

17 How many more marbles does
Sasha have than Claire? _____

18 How many fewer marbles does
Claire have than Sasha? _____

Rocky has 7 fishing lures. Megan has
12 fishing lures.

19 How many fewer fishing lures does
Rocky have than Megan? _____

Comparison Problems

Comparison Problems With an Unknown Larger or Smaller Amount

Solve each problem. Label your answers.

Show your work.

20 Unknown Larger Amount Maribel has 18 stickers. Arnon has 13 more stickers than Maribel. How many stickers does Arnon have?

_____

21 Unknown Smaller Amount Arnon has 31 stickers. Maribel has 13 fewer stickers than Arnon. How many stickers does Maribel have?

_____

22 Unknown Larger Amount Ivan has 19 goldfish. Milo has 15 more goldfish than Ivan. How many goldfish does Milo have?

_____

23 Unknown Smaller Amount Milo has 34 goldfish. Ivan has 15 fewer goldfish than Milo. How many goldfish does Ivan have?

_____

Use Comparison Bars to Represent an Unknown Amount

Solve each problem. Label your answers.

Show your work.

24 Unknown Smaller Amount T.J. has 18 fewer miniature cars than Corey. Corey has 32 miniature cars. How many miniature cars does T.J. have?

_____

25 Unknown Larger Amount Corey has 18 more miniature cars than T.J. T.J. has 14 miniature cars. How many miniature cars does Corey have?

_____

26 Unknown Smaller Amount Grace has 19 fewer stuffed animals than Sophia. Sophia has 31 stuffed animals. How many stuffed animals does Grace have?

_____

27 Unknown Larger Amount Sophia has 19 more stuffed animals than Grace. Grace has 12 stuffed animals. How many stuffed animals does Sophia have?

_____

✓**Check Understanding**

Jen has 14 more dolls than Avery. Avery has 16 dolls. Draw comparison bars to find the number of dolls Jen has.

Comparison Problems

Name _____

What's the Error?

Dear Math Students,

As part of my math homework, I solved this problem:

Carlos has 19 fish. He has 14 fewer fish than Daniel. How many fish does Daniel have?

Here is what I did: 19 − 14 = 5

Is my answer right? If not, please correct my work, and tell me what I did wrong.

Your friend,
Puzzled Penguin

Daniel has 5 fish.

Carlos	19
Daniel	? (14)

1 Write an answer to Puzzled Penguin.

_____

_____

Solve Comparison Problems with Misleading Language

Solve each problem on a separate piece of paper.

2 Unknown Smaller Amount
Daniel has 23 fish. He has 15 more fish than Carlos. How many fish does Carlos have?

3 Unknown Larger Amount
Gina ran 12 laps. She ran 8 fewer laps than Bettina. How many laps did Bettina run?

4 Unknown Smaller Amount
Bettina ran 20 laps. She ran 8 more laps than Gina. How many laps did Gina run?

5 Unknown Larger Amount
Sara read 18 books this year. She read 13 fewer books than Lupe. How many books did Lupe read this year?

Solve Comparison Problems Without the Words *More* or *Fewer*

Solve each problem. Label your answers.

Show your work.

6 The coach brought 18 hockey sticks to practice. There were 23 players at practice. How many players didn't get sticks?

_____

7 At a meeting, 15 people had to stand because there were not enough chairs. There were 12 chairs. How many people came to the meeting?

_____

8 At the park, 4 of the children could not swing because there were not enough swings. There were 20 children at the park. How many swings were on the swing set?

_____

9 Maile took one step on each tile along the garden path. After she took 14 steps, there were 13 more tiles left to go. How many tiles were there along the path?

_____

✓ Check Understanding

Rewrite the comparison statement "Pete has 12 fewer tools than Cooper" using the word *more*.

_____

Comparison Problems with Misleading Language

Solve Problems with Extra Information

Read each problem. Cross out any extra information. Then solve.

1 Emma solved 9 math problems and answered 7 reading questions. Her sister solved 8 math problems. How many math problems did they solve in all?

_____

2 Mark had 6 shirts and 5 pairs of pants. Today his aunt gave him 4 more shirts and another pair of pants. How many shirts does he have now?

_____

3 A parking lot had 179 cars and 95 trucks. Then 85 cars left the lot. How many cars are in the parking lot now?

_____

4 Laura had some roses in a vase. From her garden, she picked 7 more roses and 6 daisies. Now she has 12 roses in all. How many roses did she have at first?

_____

5 Nikko had 245 pennies and 123 nickels. His brother gave him 89 more pennies and 25 more nickels. How many pennies does Nikko have now?

_____

© Houghton Mifflin Harcourt Publishing Company

Solve Problems with Hidden Information

**Read each problem. Circle the hidden information.
Then solve.**

6 Samuel had 16 new horseshoes in the shed yesterday. Today, he put a new set of horseshoes on his horse Betsy. How many horseshoes are left in the shed?

_____

7 Maya is going on a vacation with her family for a week and 3 days. How many days will she be on vacation?

_____

8 Julie bought a dozen eggs at the market. She gave 3 of them to Serge. How many eggs does Julie have left?

_____

9 Lisa had 3 quarters and 2 dimes. Then she found 3 nickels and 12 pennies. What is the value of the coins in cents she has now?

_____

10 Marissa is moving away. She is going to move back in 1 year and 21 days. How many days will she be gone?

_____

Name _____

Recognize Word Problems with Not Enough Information

Tell what information is needed to solve each problem.

11 Sara bought 8 bananas at the fruit market. She put them in a bowl with some oranges. How many pieces of fruit are in the bowl?

_____

_____

12 Rebecca did 112 dives in competition last summer. This summer, she did many more dives in competition. How many competition dives did she do in the two summers?

_____

_____

13 Meg bought 3 mystery books and put them on the shelf with her other mystery books. How many mystery books are now on the shelf?

_____

_____

14 Our school has 5 soccer balls, 6 basketballs, and 4 footballs. Today, some of the footballs were lost. How many balls does the school have now?

_____

_____

Solve Word Problems with Not Enough Information

If more information is needed, rewrite the problem to include the necessary information. Then solve it.

Show your work.

15 Leah began fishing at 2:00 P.M. She stopped at dinnertime. How many hours did Leah fish?

_____

_____

16 The train traveled 376 miles on Thursday. It traveled even more miles on Friday. How many miles did the train travel on the two days?

_____

_____

17 The Kitchen Store sold 532 pans and 294 pots. Then some pans were returned. How many pans were not returned?

_____

_____

18 Julio and Scott played 6 card games and 4 computer games today. How many hours did they play games?

_____

_____

✓ **Check Understanding**

Write extra information from a problem above that is not needed to solve the problem. _____

_____

Solve the problem. Label your answer.

Show your work.

1 Marie drove 43 miles. Sherry drove 15 miles. How many more miles did Marie drive than Sherry?

_____

2 George had some money in his wallet. He spent $35 but still has $27 left. How much money did he have in his wallet before he spent any of it?

_____

3 There are 63 potatoes in a sack. There are 29 rotten potatoes in the sack. How many are not rotten?

_____

4 Jessica scored 38 points fewer than Elizabeth. Jessica scored 54 points. How many points did Elizabeth score?

_____

Read the problem. Circle the hidden information. Then solve.

5 Omar buys a dozen oranges at the market. He uses 5 of them to make juice. How many oranges does Omar have left?

_____

Name _____ Date _____

Multiply or divide.

1 $4 \times 1 = \boxed{}$

2 $2 \div 1 = \boxed{}$

3 $3 \times 2 = \boxed{}$

4 $9 \div 3 = \boxed{}$

5 $5 \times 6 = \boxed{}$

6 $24 \div 4 = \boxed{}$

7 $8 \times 5 = \boxed{}$

8 $63 \div 7 = \boxed{}$

9 $9 \times 9 = \boxed{}$

Add or subtract.

10
$$\begin{array}{r} 478 \\ -\ 265 \\ \hline \end{array}$$

11
$$\begin{array}{r} 243 \\ +\ 536 \\ \hline \end{array}$$

12
$$\begin{array}{r} 562 \\ -\ 348 \\ \hline \end{array}$$

13
$$\begin{array}{r} 635 \\ +\ 258 \\ \hline \end{array}$$

14
$$\begin{array}{r} 824 \\ -\ 659 \\ \hline \end{array}$$

15
$$\begin{array}{r} 579 \\ +\ 323 \\ \hline \end{array}$$

Write First-Step Questions

Write the first-step question and answer. Then solve the problem.

Show your work.

1. The orchard has 8 rows of apple trees. There are 7 rows with 6 apple trees and one row with 4 apple trees. How many apple trees are in the orchard?

_____

_____

2. Ms. Hayes bought 4 packs of pencils with 10 pencils in each pack. She divided the pencils evenly among her 5 children. How many pencils did each child get?

_____

_____

3. Kylen made 30 necklaces and gave 6 away. She put the rest in 4 boxes with an equal number in each box. How many necklaces were in each box?

_____

_____

4. Libby had 42 vacation pictures and 12 birthday pictures. She put an equal number of pictures in 9 photo folders. How many pictures did she put in each photo folder?

_____

_____

5. Mr. Cerda bought 9 boxes of tiles. Each box had 8 tiles. He used all but 5 of the tiles. How many tiles did Mr. Cerda use?

_____

_____

© Houghton Mifflin Harcourt Publishing Company

Write First-Step Questions (continued)

**Write the first-step question and answer.
Then solve the problem.**

Show your work.

6 A bus has 10 seats that can each hold 2 passengers and another seat that can hold 3 passengers. How many passengers can be seated on the bus?

_____

_____

7 Dana made 6 fruit baskets. She put 4 apples, 2 pears, and 3 oranges in each basket. How many pieces of fruit did Dana use in all?

_____

_____

8 Cecilia ordered 5 pizzas for a group of friends. Each pizza had 8 slices. All but 3 slices were eaten. How many slices were eaten?

_____

_____

9 Randall has 122 coins in his collection. He has 50 coins that are quarters and the rest are nickels. If he fills 9 pages in a coin folder with the same number of nickels, how many nickels are on each page?

_____

_____

✓**Check Understanding**

Explain how you know a problem is a two-step problem.

Name _____

What's the Error?

Dear Math Students,

My teacher gave me this problem:

Luther had 11 sheets of color paper. There were 6 orange sheets, and the rest were blue. Today he used 2 sheets of blue paper. How many sheets of blue paper does Luther have now?

Here is what I did: 11 − 6 = 5
Luther now has 5 blue sheets.

Is my answer correct? If not, please correct my work and tell me what I did wrong.

Your friend,
Puzzled Penguin

1 Write an answer to Puzzled Penguin.

_____

Solve Two-Step Word Problems

Solve each problem. Label your answers.

2 The bus had 14 passengers. When it stopped, 5 people got off and 8 people got on. How many people are riding the bus now?

_____

3 There are 15 fish in a tank. 12 have stripes, and the others are do not. How many more striped fish are there than fish without stripes?

_____

Solve and Discuss

Solve each problem. Label your answers.

4 Sun Mi picked 14 apricots. Celia picked 5 fewer apricots than Sun Mi. How many apricots did Sun Mi and Celia pick altogether?

5 Annie took 8 photographs at home and 7 photographs at school. Her sister Amanda took 6 fewer photographs than Annie. How many photographs did Amanda take?

6 There are 5 sheep, 3 goats, and some rabbits in the petting zoo. Altogether there are 15 animals in the petting zoo. How many rabbits are there?

7 A new library opened on Saturday. The library lent out 234 books on Saturday. On Sunday, they lent out 138 books. By the end of the weekend, 78 books were returned. How many books were not returned?

8 Katie had 8 dimes and some nickels in her duck bank. She had 4 more nickels than dimes. She took out 5 nickels to put in her coin purse. How many nickels are in her duck bank now?

9 Tony had 14 color pencils. There were 9 of them that needed to be sharpened, and the rest were sharp. Yesterday, his uncle gave him some new color pencils. Now Tony has 12 sharp color pencils. How many color pencils did his uncle give him?

Is the Answer Reasonable?

Use rounding or mental math to decide if the answer is reasonable. Write *yes* or *no*. Then write an equation and solve the problem to see if you were correct.

Show your work.

10 Chelsea's class collected cans of food for their local food pantry. They collected 27 cans on Monday and 78 cans on Tuesday. Then on Wednesday they collected 53 cans. How many cans did the class collect on those three days?
Answer: **158 cans**

_____

11 Barry strings beads. He had 54 beads on a string and he took off 29 beads. Then he took off 5 more. How many beads are on the string now?
Answer: **35 beads**

_____

12 Dena counted the books on three shelves of the classroom library. She counted 33 books on the top shelf, 52 books on the middle shelf, and 48 books on the bottom shelf. How many books are on the three shelves?
Answer: **163 books**

_____

13 Ms. Lance bought 6 packages of paper cups. Each package has 20 cups. She used 78 cups for a party. How many cups does Ms. Lance have left?
Answer: **58 cups**

_____

Reasonable Answers

**Use rounding or mental math to decide if the answer
is reasonable. Write *yes* or *no*. Then write an equation
and solve the problem to see if you were correct.**

Show your work.

14 There were 83 students in a spelling contest.
First, 9 students were eliminated. Then 29 students
were eliminated. How many students were left?
Answer: 24 students

_____

15 During one week Tina rode her bicycle 42 miles
and Jim rode 9 fewer miles than Tina. How many
miles did they ride altogether that week?
Answer: 75 miles

_____

16 It costs $10 a day to care for a cat or dog in the animal
shelter. The total cost one day was $90. There were
5 dogs at the shelter and the rest were cats. How
many cats were at the shelter that day?
Answer: 9 cats

_____

17 Jake is saving money for a bike that costs $187.
He saved $55 in April and $44 in May. How much
more money does Jake need to buy the bike?
Answer: $88

_____

Check Understanding

Explain how you decided if $88 for Problem 17 was reasonable.

© Houghton Mifflin Harcourt Publishing Company

Solve Two-Step Word Problems

Equations and Two-Step Word Problems

Write an equation and solve the problem.

Show your work.

1 Mrs. Delgado is baking pies and cakes for a school fundraiser. She bought 26 apples, 29 peaches, and a number of bananas at the Farmers' Market. She bought 66 pieces of fruit. How many bananas did she buy?

_____

2 Abby bought 8 packages of stickers with the same number of stickers in each package. She gave 15 stickers to her sister. Now Abby has 49 stickers. How many stickers were in each package?

_____

3 Taylor is reading a 340-page book. He read 174 pages of the book on Saturday and 120 pages on Sunday. How many pages does he have left to read?

_____

4 Lauren had a piece of ribbon that was 36 inches long. She cut a number of 3-inch pieces. She has 15 inches of ribbon left. How many 3-inch pieces did she cut?

_____

5 There are 47 students in the marching band. There are 5 students in the first row, and the rest are in equal rows of 6. How many students are in each of the 6 rows?

_____

Solve Two-Step Word Problems

Write an equation and solve the problem.   *Show your work.*

6 Sara baked 48 cookies and gave a dozen cookies
to her friend. She put the remaining cookies on
plates of 9 cookies each. How many plates did she use?

_____

7 Marissa is making floral bouquets. She bought
56 tulips, 73 daisies, and some roses. She bought
153 flowers in all. How many roses did she buy?

_____

8 Tom has 103 photos on his digital camera. He deletes
33 photos. He prints the remaining photos and puts
an equal number on each page of an album that has
10 pages. How many photos are on each page?

_____

9 Leo bought 6 sets of books. Each set had the same
number of books. He donated 11 books to the school
library. Now he has 37 books left. How many books
were in each set of books Leo bought?

_____

10 Amber has 5 packages of chalk. Each package has
9 pieces of chalk. She gave a number of pieces of
chalk to her brother. Amber has 37 pieces of chalk
left. How many pieces did Amber give her brother?

_____

✓**Check Understanding**
Describe the strategy you used to solve Problem 10.

Write Two-Step Equations

Write an equation and solve the problem.

1 Carrie played a video game and scored 20 points 7 times and 55 points 1 time. How many points did Carrie score?

Show your work.

2 Darin earns $8 each week doing chores. He is saving his money to buy a game that costs $49 and a cap that costs $15. How many weeks will Darin need to save his money?

3 A dog trainer is working with 7 dogs. He rewards each dog with the same number of treats. He started with 35 treats and he has 7 left. How many treats did he give each dog?

4 Sheila has two dogs. One dog weighs 46 pounds and her other dog weighs 14 pounds more. How many pounds do the two dogs weigh altogether?

5 Eli has 36 stamps and his brother has 24 stamps. They put their stamps in the same book. They put the same number of stamps on each page. They used 10 pages. How many stamps are on each page?

© Houghton Mifflin Harcourt Publishing Company

Write Two-Step Equations (continued)

Write an equation and solve the problem.

Show your work.

6 There were 9 rows of chairs set up in the school gym. Each row had 20 chairs. After the students were seated, there were 12 empty chairs. How many chairs were filled?

_____

7 Eric had 143 baseball cards. His uncle gave him a number more. Then Eric gave 26 cards to a friend. He has 184 cards now. How many cards did Eric's uncle give him?

_____

8 Brandi had 8 equal rows of stickers. She bought 5 more and now she has 53 stickers. How many were in each row before she bought more?

_____

9 Randall cut a board into two pieces. One piece has a length of 84 inches. The other piece is 24 inches shorter. How long was the board Randall cut?

_____

10 A science poster shows 9 insects with 6 legs each and a spider with 8 legs. How many legs is that altogether?

_____

✓**Check Understanding**

Explain how you decided which operations to use in your equation for Problem 10.

Practice with Two-Step Word Problems

Name

Sports Statistics in the News

Little League Baseball Championships: Wheaton Wolves Score Win

Wheaton Wolves win Little League World Series Championship. The chart shows some statistics from the six games the team played.

Wheaton Wolves Statistics	
Times at Bat	155
Hits	47
Base on Balls	25
Runs Scored	36
Strike Outs	36

Use the information in the table to write an equation and solve the problem.

1. How many times at bat did players not strike out or get a base on balls?

2. How many hits and base on balls did not result in a run?

3. The Wheaton Wolves had 13 triple or double-base hits, 3 homeruns, and the rest were single-base hits. How many single-base hits did the team get?

© Houghton Mifflin Harcourt Publishing Company • Image Credits: ©Stockbroker/MBI/Alamy

Sports News

Danielle plays on a third grade basketball team in a league. Her team made the news when they scored 47 points, 41 points, and 53 points in a three-game tournament.

Write a two-step equation and solve the problem.

4 How many points did Danielle's team score altogether?

_____

5 Describe how you can use mental math to decide if your answer to Problem 4 is reasonable.

_____

_____

_____

6 Danielle's scorecard shows her statistics for the three games. Use the information in the table to write equations to find the unknown numbers. Then complete the table.

_____

_____

	Number of 1-pt Free Throws	Number of 2-pt Field Goals	Total Points
Game 1	5	7	
Game 2		6	18
Game 3	3		21

Focus on Mathematical Practices

Complete.

Show your work.

1 Lila makes bags of stickers that are exactly the same for 5 friends. She uses a total of 45 stickers. Each bag has 2 butterfly stickers and the rest are flower stickers. How many flower stickers are in each bag? Write a first-step question and answer. Then solve the problem.

_____

_____

2 Troy saves money for a bike that costs $126. He saves $58 one month and $43 the next month. How much more money does Troy need to buy the bike?
Answer: $15
Is the answer reasonable? Explain.

_____

3 The Downtown bus has 16 passengers. When it stops, 4 people get off and 7 people get on. How many passengers are on the Downtown bus now?

_____

Write an equation and solve the problem.

4 Lauren has 109 rare coins. She sells 37 coins. She wants to put the rest of the coins in an album. Each page in the album holds 8 coins. How many pages will she use?

_____

_____

5 Peyton cuts a pipe into two pieces. One piece has a length of 13 feet. The other piece is 9 feet shorter. How long was the pipe Peyton cut?

_____

_____

Name _____ **Date** _____

PATH to
FLUENCY

Multiply or divide.

1 $4 \div 2 = $ ☐

2 $2 \times 4 = $ ☐

3 $72 \div 8 = $ ☐

4 $3 \times 8 = $ ☐

5 $25 \div 5 = $ ☐

6 $8 \times 4 = $ ☐

7 $40 \div 8 = $ ☐

8 $9 \times 6 = $ ☐

9 $80 \div 8 = $ ☐

Add or subtract.

10
```
  211
+ 167
```

11
```
  472
- 231
```

12
```
  527
+ 268
```

13
```
  682
- 537
```

14
```
  636
+ 289
```

15
```
  911
- 685
```

1 Mr. Taylor arranges some chairs in rows. He puts the same number of chairs in each of 7 rows and puts 7 chairs in the last row. He sets up 70 chairs. How many chairs does he put in each of the 7 equal rows?

Choose the equation that can be used to solve the problem.

I can use the equation

$$(7 \times c) + 7 = 70$$

$$(70 \div 7) + 7 = c$$

$$(7 \times c) - 7 = 70$$

.

Solve the problem.

_____ chairs

2 Marisol picks 150 flowers. She picks 80 red flowers and the rest are yellow. She sells 45 yellow flowers. How many yellow flowers does she have now?

For numbers 2a–2e, choose Yes or No to tell whether the equation can be used to find the number of yellow flowers Marisol has now.

2a. $150 - 80 - 45 = y$ ○ Yes   ○ No

2b. $150 + 80 - 45 = y$ ○ Yes   ○ No

2c. $150 + 80 + 45 = y$ ○ Yes   ○ No

2d. $150 = 80 + 45 + y$ ○ Yes   ○ No

2e. $150 = 80 - 45 + y$ ○ Yes   ○ No

3 Mark makes 18 picture frames this month. He makes 7 fewer picture frames than Sara. How many picture frames does Sara make?

Draw comparison bars to represent the problem. Then solve.

_____ picture frames

4 David and Marne pick cucumbers at a farm. David picks 93 cucumbers. How many cucumbers does Marne pick?

What information is not helpful for solving the problem?

Ⓐ how many more cucumbers David picks

Ⓑ how many fewer cucumbers Marne picks

Ⓒ how many cucumbers are grown at the farm each year

Ⓓ how many cucumbers David and Marne pick

Rewrite the problem to include the necessary information. Then solve it.

5 There are 240 boys and girls in a soccer league. There are 130 girls. How many boys are there?

Write an equation with a variable to represent the problem. Then draw a Math Mountain to solve the problem.

_____ boys

6 On Wednesday, Jonah sees 30 birds and 4 rabbits. Of the birds, 13 are robins and the rest are pigeons. On Thursday, he sees some more pigeons. He has now seen 21 pigeons. How many pigeons did he see on Thursday?

Part A Write the information in the correct box.

| 30 birds | 4 rabbits | 13 robins | 21 pigeons |

Needed Information	Extra Information

Part B Solve the problem. What strategy did you use? How did it help?

7 Susan buys 24 postcards. She sends 6 postcards to friends. She puts the rest in 3 folders, with an equal number in each folder. How many postcards are in each folder?

Write the first step question and answer. Then solve.

_____ postcards

8 Kato uses 56 photos to make online albums. He puts 7 photos in each album. How many albums does Kato make?

For Exercises 8a–8d, select True or False if the equation can be used to solve the problem.

8a. $7 \times a = 56$ ○ True   ○ False

8b. $56 \div 7 = a$ ○ True   ○ False

8c. $7 \times 56 = a$ ○ True   ○ False

8d. $56 \div a = 7$ ○ True   ○ False

9 Tara posts 35 flyers for the school carnival. Keisha posts 8 more flyers than Tara. How many flyers did Tara and Keisha post? Choose the number that completes the sentence.

Tara and Keisha post | 43 / 62 / 78 | flyers.

10 Jason packs 54 grapefruit in 9 boxes for shipping. He packs the same number of grapefruit in each box. How many grapefruit does Jason pack into each box?

Use the numbers and symbols to write a situation equation and a solution equation. Then solve.

| g | 9 | 54 | × | ÷ | = |

Situation Equation: _____

Solution Equation: _____

_____ grapefruit

11 Declan reads 19 books. He reads 13 fewer books than Ellie. How many books does Ellie read?

_____ books

12 Parker has 452 toy dinosaurs in his collection. His sister gives him 38 more toy dinosaurs. Then he sells some of them online. Parker now has 418 toy dinosaurs. How many did he sell?

Answer: 72 toy dinosaurs

Is the answer reasonable? Tell why or why not. Then write an equation and solve the problem.

13 Eva buys some items at the store and pays with pennies and nickels. Use the information in the table to write equations to find the unknown numbers. Then complete the table.

Pencil: _____

Eraser: _____

Clip: _____

	Number of Pennies	Number of Nickels	Total Cost
Pencil	6	8	¢
Eraser		4	24¢
Clip	2		37¢

14 Holly is going to the beach in 2 weeks and 4 days.

Which equation can be used to find the number of days until Holly goes to the beach?

Ⓐ $2 \times 7 + 4 = b$; $b = 18$ days

Ⓑ $2 \times 5 + 4 = b$; $b = 14$ days

Ⓒ $2 + 7 + 4 = b$; $b = 13$ days

Ⓓ $2 \times 7 - 4 = b$; $b = 10$ days

15 Omar has 5 ties and Ryan has 12 ties. How many more ties does Ryan have than Omar?

Make a comparison drawing to represent the problem. Then solve.

_____ more ties

Planning a Garden

Last year community gardeners planted 8 rows of
tomato plants with the same number in each row.
Then they planted 10 more plants. There was a total of
58 plants. How many plants were in each row before
they planted the additional 10?

1 Write an equation to represent the problem. Solve.

2 Could you write an equation for the problem using
other operations than the ones you used?
Explain why or why not.

3 Gardeners decided to buy stakes to help support
the tomato plants. The stakes are sold in bundles
of 12. If the gardeners bought 5 bundles of stakes,
did they buy enough stakes? How many more do
they need or how many extras do they have? Write
an equation to solve. Explain the solution.

4 Community gardeners plan to plant pumpkins this year. Write a two-step word problem about planting pumpkins that can be solved using an equation. Solve and explain the solution.

5 The gardeners plan to plant 40 pumpkin plants. They have space for 7 rows. They would like to keep an equal number of pumpkin plants in each row, if possible. Draw a picture to show the number of pumpkin plants they should plant in each row. Write an equation to match your picture.

6 How would the garden change if gardeners planted the pumpkin plants in 8 rows?

Dear Family:

In this unit, students explore ways to measure things using the customary and metric systems of measurement.

The units of measure we will be working with include:

U.S. Customary System

Capacity
1 cup (c) = 8 fluid ounces (oz)
1 pint (pt) = 2 cups (c)
1 quart (qt) = 2 pints (pt)
1 gallon (gal) = 4 quarts (qt)
Weight
1 pound (lb) = 16 ounces (oz)

Metric System

Capacity
1 liter (L) = 1,000 milliliters (mL)
Mass
1 kilogram (kg) = 1,000 grams (g)

Students will solve problems that involve liquid volumes or masses given in the same unit by adding, subtracting, multiplying, or dividing and by using a drawing to represent the problem.

You can help your child become familiar with these units of measure by working with measurements together. For example, you might use a measuring cup to explore how the cup can be used to fill pints, quarts, or gallons of liquid.

Thank you for helping your child learn important math skills. Please contact me, if you have any questions or comments.

Sincerely,
Your child's teacher

Unit 7 addresses the following standards from the Common Core State Standards for Mathematics: **3.OA.3, 3.MD.A.2, 3.G.A.1, 3.G.A.2, 3.MD.C.5, 3.MD.C.5.a, 3.MD.C.5.b, 3.MD.C.6, 3.MD.C.7, 3.MD.C.7.a, 3.MD.C.7.b, 3.MD.C.7.c, 3.MD.C.7.d, 3.MD.D.8** and all Mathematical Practices.

Estimada familia:

En esta unidad los niños estudian cómo medir cosas usando el sistema usual de medidas y el sistema métrico decimal.

Las unidades de medida con las que trabajaremos incluirán:

Sistema usual

Capacidad
1 taza (tz) = 8 onzas líquidas (oz)
1 pinta (pt) = 2 tazas (tz)
1 cuarto (ct) = 2 pintas (pt)
1 galón (gal) = 4 cuartos (ct)

Peso
1 libra (lb) = 16 onzas (oz)

Sistema métrico decimal

Capacidad
1 litro (L) = 1,000 mililitros (mL)

Masa
1 kilogramo (kg) = 1,000 gramos (g)

Los estudiantes resolverán problemas relacionados con volúmenes de líquido o masas, que se dan en la misma unidad, sumando, restando o dividiendo, y usando un dibujo para representar el problema.

Puede ayudar a que su niño se familiarice con estas unidades de medida midiendo con él diversas cosas. Por ejemplo, podrían usar una taza de medidas para aprender cómo se pueden llenar pintas, cuartos o galones con líquido.

Gracias por ayudar a su niño a aprender destrezas matemáticas importantes. Si tiene alguna duda o algún comentario, por favor comuníquese conmigo.

Atentamente,
El maestro de su niño

En la Unidad 7 se aplican los siguientes estándares de los Estándares estatales comunes de matemáticas: **3.OA.3, 3.MD.A.2, 3.G.A.1, 3.G.A.2, 3.MD.C.5, 3.MD.C.5.a, 3.MD.C.5.b, 3.MD.C.6, 3.MD.C.7, 3.MD.C.7.a, 3.MD.C.7.b, 3.MD.C.7.c, 3.MD.C.7.d, 3.MD.D.8,** y todos los de Prácticas matemáticas.

adjacent sides

convex

angle

cup (c)

concave

decagon

A polygon is convex if all of its diagonals are inside it.

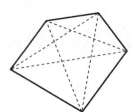

Two sides of a figure that meet at a point.

Example:
Sides *a* and *b* are adjacent.

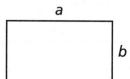

A customary unit of measure used to measure capacity.

1 cup = 8 fluid ounces
2 cups = 1 pint
4 cups = 1 quart
16 cups = 1 gallon

A figure formed by two rays or two line segments that meet at an endpoint.

A polygon with 10 sides.

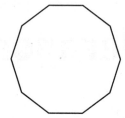

A polygon for which you can connect two points inside the polygon with a segment that passes outside the polygon.

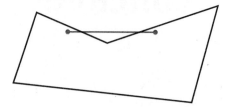

fluid ounce (fl oz)	hexagon
gallon (gal)	kilogram (kg)
gram (g)	liquid volume

A polygon with six sides.

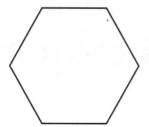

A unit of liquid volume in the customary system that equals $\frac{1}{8}$ cup or 2 tablespoons.

A metric unit of mass.

1 kilogram = 1,000 grams

A customary unit used to measure capacity.

1 gallon = 4 quarts = 8 pints = 16 cups

A measure of how much a container can hold. Also called *capacity.*

A metric unit of mass.
One paper clip has a mass of about 1 gram.

1,000 grams = 1 kilogram

liter (L)

octagon

mass

opposite sides

milliliter (mL)

ounce (oz)

A polygon with eight sides.

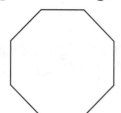

A metric unit used to measure capacity.

1 liter = 1,000 milliliters

Sides of a polygon that are across from each other; they do not meet at a point.

Example:

Sides *a* and *c* are opposite.

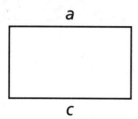

The amount of matter in an object.

A customary unit used to measure weight.

16 ounces = 1 pound

A metric unit used to measure capacity.

1,000 milliliters = 1 liter

parallelogram

polygon

pentagon

pound (lb)

pint (pt)

quadrilateral

A closed plane figure with sides made up of straight line segments.

A quadrilateral with both pairs of opposite sides parallel.

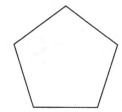

A customary unit used to measure weight.

1 pound = 16 ounces

A polygon with five sides.

A polygon with four sides.

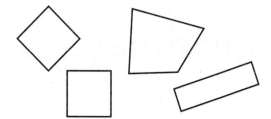

A customary unit used to measure capacity.

1 pint = 2 cups

quart (qt)

rhombus

ray

right angle

rectangle

square

A parallelogram with equal sides.

A customary unit used to measure capacity.

1 quart = 4 cups

An angle that measures 90°.

A part of a line that has one endpoint and goes on forever in one direction.

A rectangle with four sides of the same length.

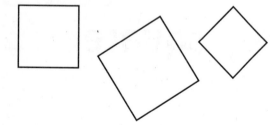

A parallelogram that has 4 right angles.

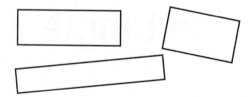

trapezoid

triangle

weight

A quadrilateral with exactly one pair of parallel sides.

A polygon with three sides.

The measure of how heavy something is.

Name _____

Choose the Unit

Choose the best unit to use to measure the liquid volume. Write *cup*, *pint*, *quart*, or *gallon*.

1 a carton of heavy cream

_____

2 a flower vase

_____

3 a swimming pool

_____

4 a wash tub

_____

What's the Error?

Dear Math Students,

Today I had to choose the best unit to use to measure how much water is needed to fill a kitchen sink. I said the best unit to use is cups. Is my answer correct? If not, please correct my work and tell me what I did wrong.

Your friend,
Puzzled Penguin

5 Write an answer to Puzzled Penguin.

_____

_____

_____

6 **Math Journal** Think of a container. Choose the unit you would use to measure its capacity. Draw the container and write the name of the unit you chose. Explain why you chose that unit.

Estimate Customary Units of Liquid Volume

Ring the better estimate.

2 cups

2 quarts

5 cups

5 gallons

1 pint

1 gallon

1 cup

1 pint

1 cup

1 gallon

30 cups

30 gallons

Solve.

13 Jamie makes a shopping list for a picnic with his four friends.
He estimates that he'll need 5 quarts of lemonade for the group
to drink. Do you think his estimate is reasonable? Explain.

_____

_____

_____

Use Drawings to Solve Problems

Use the drawing to represent and solve the problem.

14 A painter mixed 5 pints of yellow and 3 pints of blue paint to make green paint. How many pints of green paint did he make?

_____

15 Ryan bought a bottle of orange juice that had 16 fluid ounces. He poured 6 fluid ounces in a cup. How many fluid ounces are left in the bottle?

_____

16 A restaurant made 8 quarts of tea. They used all the tea to fill pitchers that hold 2 quarts each. How many pitchers were filled with tea?

_____

17 An ice cream machine makes 5 pints of ice cream in a batch. If 3 batches were made, how many pints of ice cream were made?

_____

18 Fran has a water jug that holds 24 quarts of water. She fills it with a container that holds 4 quarts. How many times must she fill the 4-quart container and pour it into the jug to fill the jug with 24 quarts?

_____

Solve Problems

Use the drawing to represent and solve the problem.

Show your work.

19 Shanna bought 8 juice boxes filled with her favorite juice. Each box holds 10 fluid ounces. How many fluid ounces of her favorite juice did Shanna buy?

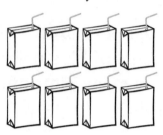

_____

20 Juana filled her punch bowl with 12 cups of punch. She gave some of her friends each a cup of punch. There are 7 cups of punch left in the bowl. How many cups did she give to friends?

_____

21 Mrs. Chavez made 20 quarts of pickles. She made 4 quarts each day. How many days did it take her to make the pickles?

_____

22 A mid-sized aquarium holds 25 gallons of water and a large aquarium holds 35 gallons of water. How many gallons of water is needed to fill both aquariums?

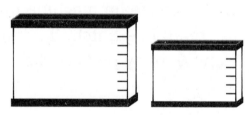

_____

Check Understanding

Name the 5 units of liquid volume in this lesson from largest to smallest.

_____ , _____ , _____ ,

_____ , _____

Customary Units of Liquid Volume

Name _____

Choose the Appropriate Unit

Choose the unit you would use to measure the liquid volume of each. Write *mL* or *L*.

1. a kitchen sink _____

2. a soup spoon _____

3. a teacup _____

4. a washing machine _____

Circle the better estimate.

5. a juice container   1 L   1 mL

6. a bowl of soup   500 L   500 mL

Use Drawings to Represent Problems

Use the drawing to represent and solve the problem.

7. There were 900 milliliters of water in a pitcher. Terri poured 500 milliliters of water into a bowl. How many milliliters of water are left in the pitcher?

   _____

8. Mr. Rojo put 6 liters of fuel into a gas can that can hold 10 liters. Then he added more liters to fill the can. How many liters of fuel did he add to the can?

   _____

9. Shelby needs to water each of her 3 plants with 200 milliliters of water. How many milliliters of water does she need?

   _____

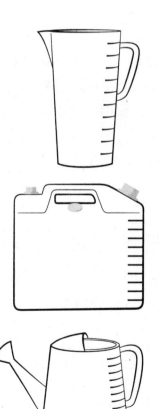

Make Sense of Problems Involving Liquid Volume

Use the drawing to represent and solve the problem.

10 The deli sold 24 liters of juice in 3 days. The same amount was sold each day. How many liters of juice did the deli sell each day?

_____

11 Tim has a bucket filled with 12 liters of water and a bucket filled with 20 liters of water. What is the total liquid volume of the buckets?

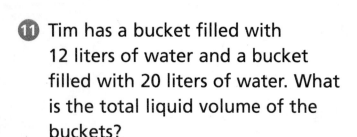

_____

12 Sara made a smoothie and gave her friend 250 milliliters. There are 550 milliliters left. How many milliliters of smoothie did Sara make?

_____

Solve. Use a drawing if you need to.

13 Diane has 36 cups of tea to divide equally among 4 tables. How many cups should she put at each table?

_____

14 Mr. Valle filled 7 jars with his famous barbeque sauce. Each jar holds 2 pints. How many pints of sauce did he have?

_____

✓ **Check Understanding**

Describe the relationship between a liter and a milliliter.

Metric Units of Liquid Volume

Choose the Appropriate Unit

VOCABULARY
weight
pound (lb)
ounce (oz)

Choose the unit you would use to measure the weight of each. Write *pound or ounce*.

1 a backpack full of books

_____

2 a couch

_____

3 a peanut

_____

4 a pencil

_____

Circle the better estimate.

5 a student desk   3 lb   30 lb

6 a television   20 oz   20 lb

7 a hamster   5 oz   5 lb

8 a slice of cheese 1 lb   1 oz

Use Drawings to Represent Problems

Use the drawing to represent and solve the problem.

9 Selma filled each of 3 bags with 5 ounces of her favorite nuts. How many ounces of nuts did she use altogether to fill the bags?

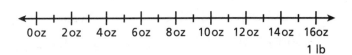

0oz 2oz 4oz 6oz 8oz 10oz 12oz 14oz 16oz
                                              1 lb

_____

10 Two apples together weigh 16 ounces. If one apple weighs 9 ounces, how much does the other apple weigh?

0oz 2oz 4oz 6oz 8oz 10oz 12oz 14oz 16oz
                                              1 lb

_____

Use Drawings to Represent Problems (continued)

Use the drawing to represent and solve the problem.

11 Noah bought 16 ounces of turkey meat. If he uses 4 ounces to make a turkey patty, how many patties can he make?

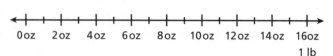

_____

12 A package of silver beads weighs 6 ounces and a package of wooden beads weighs 7 ounces more. How much does the package of wooden beads weigh?

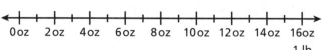

_____

Solve Word Problems

Solve. Use a drawing if you need to.

13 Ted has two dogs. Together they weigh 88 pounds. If one dog weighs 70 pounds, how much does the other dog weigh?

_____

14 Emma has 20 ounces of popcorn kernels in a bag. If she pops 4 ounces of kernels at a time, how many times can Emma pop corn?

_____

15 Susan mailed 3 packages. Each package weighed 20 ounces. What was the total weight of the 3 packages?

_____

16 Bailey caught two fish. The smaller fish weighs 14 ounces and the larger fish weighs 6 ounces more. How much does the larger fish weigh?

_____

Customary Units of Weight and Metric Units of Mass

Name _____

Choose the Appropriate Unit

VOCABULARY
mass
gram (g)
kilogram (kg)

Choose the unit you would use to measure the mass of each. Write *gram* or *kilogram*.

17 an elephant

_____

18 a crayon

_____

19 a stamp

_____

20 a dog

_____

Circle the better estimate.

21 a pair of sunglasses   150 g   150 kg

22 a horse   6 kg   600 kg

23 a watermelon   40 g   4 kg

24 a quarter   500 g   5 g

Use Drawings to Represent Problems

Use the drawing to represent and solve the problem.

25 Zach wants to buy 900 grams of pumpkin seed. The scale shows 400 grams. How many more grams does he need?

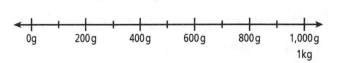

_____

26 Laura had 800 grams of fruit snacks. She put an equal amount into each of 4 containers. How many grams did she put in each container?

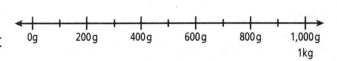

_____

Solve Word Problems

Use the drawing to represent and solve the problem.

27 Nancy used 30 grams of strawberries and 45 grams of apples in her salad. How many grams of fruit altogether did she put in her salad?

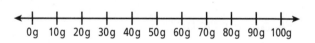

_____

28 Three people each donated a 20-kilogram bag of dog food to the animal shelter. How many kilograms of dog food was donated altogether?

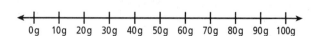

_____

Solve. Use a drawing if you need to.

29 A male leopard has a mass of 40 kilograms and a female leopard has a mass of 25 kilograms. How much more does the male weigh?

_____

30 Jolie made 3 necklaces that have a total weight of 180 grams. If each necklace weighs the same, how much would each necklace weigh?

_____

31 Dan bought 6 small bags of treats for his dog. Each bag has a weight of 40 grams. What is the total weight of all the bags?

_____

32 Carrie has a dog and a cat. Together they have a mass of 21 kilograms. If the cat has a mass of 9 kilograms, what is the mass of Carrie's dog?

_____

Customary Units of Weight and Metric Units of Mass

Name _____

What's the Error?

Dear Math Students,

Today I had to solve this problem: Toby bought 3 bags of chips. Each bag of chips weighs 50 grams. What is the weight of all 3 bags of chips? Here is how I solved the problem.

50 + 3 = 53; 53 grams

Is my answer correct? If not, please correct my work and tell me what I did wrong. How do you know my answer is wrong?

Your friend,
Puzzled Penguin

33 Write an answer to the Puzzled Penguin.

_____

_____

_____

_____

Solve. Show your work on a separate sheet of paper.

34 A tennis ball weighs 60 grams. A golf ball weighs 45 grams. How many grams do the tennis ball and golf ball weigh altogether?

35 How many more grams does the tennis ball weigh than the golf ball?

36 Gary bought 10 slices of ham at the deli. Each slice weighed 2 ounces. How many ounces of ham did Gary buy?

37 Sadie had 40 grams of sunflower seeds. She divided the seeds evenly among her 5 friends. How many grams did each friend get?

Customary Units of Weight and Metric Units of Mass **413**

Choose the Better Estimate

Circle the better estimate.

200 grams

200 kilograms

100 pounds

10 ounces

3 ounces

3 pounds

10 kilograms

10 grams

100 pounds

1 ton

1 kilogram

10 kilograms

Solve.

 Suzie explained that smaller objects weigh the least and larger objects weigh the most. Do you agree with Suzie?

_____

_____

✔ **Check Understanding**

Explain the strategies you used to estimate mass in **Problem 38.**

Customary Units of Weight and Metric Units of Mass

Name _____

Make Sense of Problems About Liquid Volume

Solve. Use drawings if you need to.

Show your work.

1   Fran works in a science lab. She poured
    80 milliliters of liquid into each of 4 test tubes.
    How many milliliters of liquid did Fran pour into
    the test tubes altogether?

    _____

2   Nicholas wants to buy a bottle of shampoo.
    A large bottle has 375 milliliters of shampoo and
    a small bottle has 250 milliliters of shampoo.
    How many more milliliters of shampoo is in the
    larger bottle?

    _____

3   Allison used two containers of water to fill her
    aquarium. She used a container filled with 18 liters
    of water and another with 12 liters of water.
    What is the total liquid volume of the aquarium?

    _____

4   The coffee shop made 28 liters of hot chocolate.
    If the same amount is poured into 4 different
    containers, how many liters of hot chocolate are in
    each container?

    _____

5   A recipe calls for 50 milliliters of milk. Eva has a
    spoon that holds 10 milliliters. How many times will
    Eva need to fill the spoon to follow the recipe?

    _____

© Houghton Mifflin Harcourt Publishing Company

Make Sense of Problems About Masses

Solve. Use drawings if you need to.

Show your work.

6 A bag of green beans has a mass of 335 grams. A bag of peas has a mass of 424 grams. What is the total mass of both bags?

_____

7 An average sized chicken egg has a mass of 60 grams. What would be the total mass of a half dozen eggs?

_____

8 A kangaroo and her joey together have a mass of 75 kilograms. If the mother kangaroo has a mass of 69 kilograms, what is the mass of the joey?

_____

9 Liam and 2 of his friends have backpacks. The backpacks have masses of 6 kilograms, 4 kilograms, and 5 kilograms. What is the total mass of the 3 backpacks?

_____

10 Graham bought 4 bags of sunflower seeds. Each bag has 60 grams of seeds. Luke bought 3 bags of pumpkin seeds. Each bag has 80 grams of seeds. Who bought more grams of seeds, Graham or Luke? Explain.

_____

✓ Check Understanding

Write and solve an equation for Problem 8.

_____

Solve Word Problems Involving Liquid Volume and Mass

Write the correct answer.

1. What would be the better unit to use to specify the mass of a large truck, grams or kilograms?

   _____

2. What would be the better unit to use to specify the volume of water you can hold in your hand, liters or milliliters?

   _____

Solve.

Show your work.

3. A pack of 6 markers weighs 48 grams. How much does 1 marker weigh?

   _____

4. It takes 15 liters of paint to paint the house. I have used 8 liters so far. How many more liters of paint will I need to finish painting the house?

   _____

5. A boy with a mass of 50 kilograms is riding on a surfboard with a mass of 15 kilograms. What is the mass of the boy and surfboard altogether?

   _____

Name _____ **Date** _____

PATH to FLUENCY

Multiply or divide.

1 $3 \div 1 =$ ☐

2 $2 \times 6 =$ ☐

3 $18 \div 3 =$ ☐

4 $6 \times 8 =$ ☐

5 $32 \div 4 =$ ☐

6 $7 \times 10 =$ ☐

7 $42 \div 7 =$ ☐

8 $7 \times 9 =$ ☐

9 $72 \div 8 =$ ☐

Add or subtract.

10
$$\begin{array}{r} 112 \\ + 834 \\ \hline \end{array}$$

11
$$\begin{array}{r} 650 \\ - 300 \\ \hline \end{array}$$

12
$$\begin{array}{r} 534 \\ + 307 \\ \hline \end{array}$$

13
$$\begin{array}{r} 843 \\ - 478 \\ \hline \end{array}$$

14
$$\begin{array}{r} 354 \\ + 618 \\ \hline \end{array}$$

15
$$\begin{array}{r} 903 \\ - 648 \\ \hline \end{array}$$

Dear Family:

Your student will be learning about geometry and measurement during this school year. The second part of Unit 7 is about triangles and the geometric figures called quadrilaterals. These get their name because they have four (*quad-*) sides (*-lateral*).

Here are some examples of quadrilaterals students will be learning about in this unit.

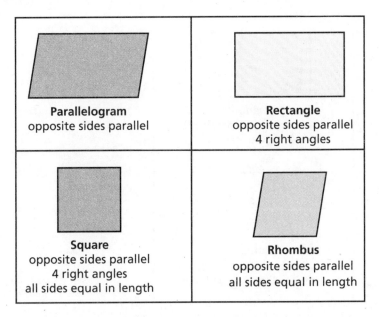

Parallelogram
opposite sides parallel

Rectangle
opposite sides parallel
4 right angles

Square
opposite sides parallel
4 right angles
all sides equal in length

Rhombus
opposite sides parallel
all sides equal in length

Students will be able to recognize and describe different quadrilaterals by their sides and angles. Some sides may be of equal length. Some sides may be parallel; they do not meet no matter how far they are extended. Some sides may be perpendicular; where they meet is like the corner of a square.

If you have any questions, please call or write to me.

Thank you.

Sincerely,
Your child's teacher

Unit 7 addresses the following standards from the Common Core State Standards for Mathematics: **3.G.A.1, 3.G.A.2, 3.MD.C.5, 3.MD.C.5.a, 3.MD.C.5.b, 3.MD.C.6, 3.MD.C.7, 3.MD.C.7.a, 3.MD.C.7.b, 3.MD.C.7.c, 3.MD.C.7.d, 3.MD.D.8, 3.OA.3, 3.MD.A.2,** and all Mathematical Practices.

Estimada familia:

Durante este año escolar, su niño aprenderá acerca de geometría y medición. La segunda parte de la Unidad 7 triangulos y trata sobre las figuras geométricas llamadas cuadriláteros. Se llaman así porque tienen cuatro (*quadri-*) lados (*-lateris*).

Aquí se muestran algunos ejemplos de cuadriláteros que los estudiantes estudiarán en esta unidad.

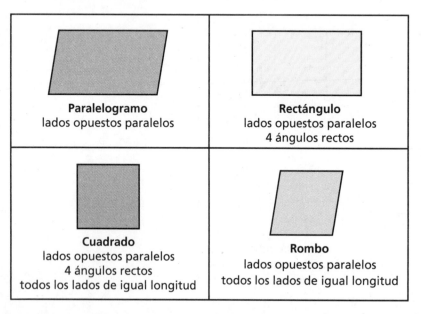

Paralelogramo	**Rectángulo**
lados opuestos paralelos	lados opuestos paralelos 4 ángulos rectos
Cuadrado	**Rombo**
lados opuestos paralelos 4 ángulos rectos todos los lados de igual longitud	lados opuestos paralelos todos los lados de igual longitud

Los estudiantes podrán reconocer y describir diferentes cuadriláteros según sus lados y ángulos. Algunos lados pueden tener la misma longitud. Algunos lados pueden ser paralelos; nunca se juntan, no importa cuánto se extiendan. Algunos lados pueden ser perpendiculares; donde se juntan es como el vértice de un cuadrado.

Si tiene alguna pregunta o algún comentario, por favor comuníquese conmigo.

Gracias.

Atentamente,
El maestro de su niño

En la Unidad 7 se aplican los siguientes estándares de los Estándares estatales comunes de matemáticas: **3.G.A.1, 3.G.A.2, 3.MD.C.5, 3.MD.C.5.a, 3.MD.C.5.b, 3.MD.C.6, 3.MD.C.7, 3.MD.C.7.a, 3.MD.C.7.b, 3.MD.C.7.c, 3.MD.C.7.d, 3.MD.D.8, 3.OA.3, 3.MD.A.2, y todos los de** Prácticas matemáticas.

Name _____

Types of Angles

A **ray** is part of a line that has one endpoint and continues forever in one direction. To draw a ray, make an arrow to show that it goes on forever.

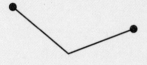

Two line segments or two rays that meet at an endpoint form an **angle**.

An angle that forms a square corner is called a **right angle**.

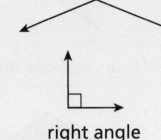

right angle

Some angles are smaller than a right angle.

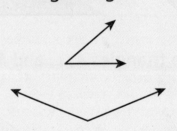

Some angles are larger than a right angle.

These angles are named with a letter in the corner.

 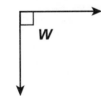 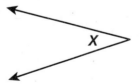 

1 Which of the angles are right angles? _____

2 Which of the angles are smaller than a right angle? _____

3 Which of the angles are larger than a right angle? _____

Describe Triangles by Types of Angles

Triangles can be described by the types of angles they have.

In these triangles, one angle is a right angle.

In these triangles, three angles are smaller than a right angle.

 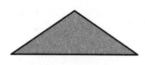  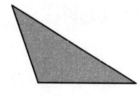

In these triangles, one angle is larger than a right angle.

  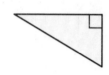 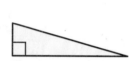

Use triangles K, L, and M for Exercises 4–6.

 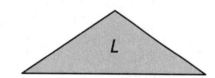 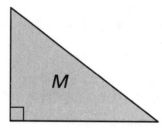

4 Which triangle has one right angle?

_____

5 Which triangle has three angles smaller than a right angle?

_____

6 Which triangle has one angle larger than a right angle?

_____

Triangles

Name _____

Describe Triangles by the Number of Sides of Equal Length

You can also describe triangles by the number of sides that are of equal length.

In these triangles, three sides are equal in length.

In these triangles, two sides are equal in length.

 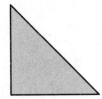 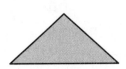

In these triangles, no sides are equal in length.

Use triangles _B_, _C_, and _D_ for Exercises 7–9.

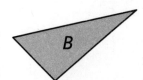 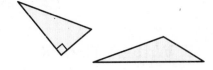

7 Which triangle has 3 sides of equal length?

_____

8 Which triangle has 2 sides of equal length?

_____

9 Which triangle has 0 sides of equal length?

_____

Describe Triangles by Types of Angles and Number of Sides of Equal Length

Use triangles M, N, and O for 10–12. Write M, N, or O. Then complete the sentences.

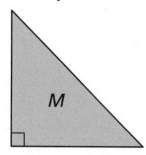

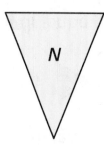

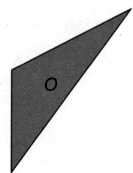

10 Triangle _____ has 1 angle larger than a right angle and has _____ sides of equal length.

11 Triangle _____ has 1 right angle and has _____ sides of equal length.

12 Triangle _____ has 3 angles smaller than a right angle and has _____ sides of equal length.

Use triangles P, Q, and R for 13–15. Write P, Q, or R. Then complete the sentences.

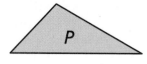

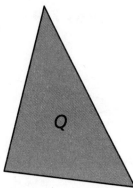

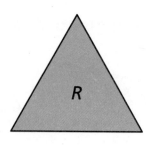

13 Triangle _____ has 3 angles smaller than a right angle and has _____ sides of equal length.

14 Triangle _____ has 3 angles smaller than a right angle and has _____ sides of equal length.

15 Triangle _____ has 1 angle larger than a right angle and has _____ sides of equal length.

Build Quadrilaterals from Triangles

A **quadrilateral** is a figure with 4 sides.

Cut out each pair of triangles. Use each pair to make as many different quadrilaterals as you can. You may flip a triangle and use the back. On a separate piece of paper, trace each quadrilateral that you make.

Triangles with One Angle Larger Than a Right Angle

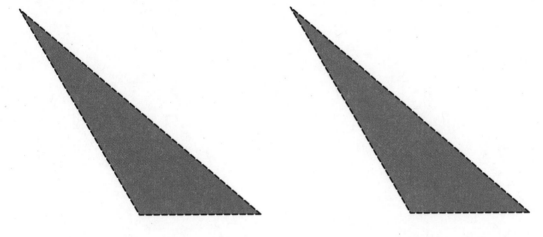

Triangles with Three Angles Smaller Than a Right Angle

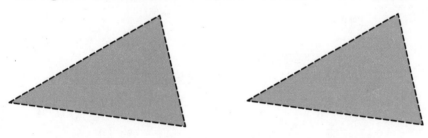

Triangles with One Right Angle

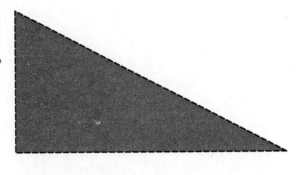
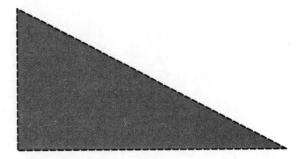

Triangles

Name _____

Polygons

A **polygon** is a flat, closed figure made up of line segments that do not cross each other.

Circle the figures that are polygons.

 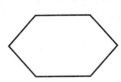   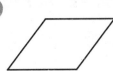

16 17 18 19

  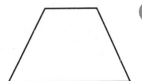 

20 21 22 23

A figure can be **concave** or **convex**. In concave polygons, there exists a line segment with endpoints inside the polygon and a point on the line segment that is outside the polygon. A convex figure has no such line segment.

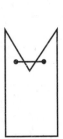 

concave   convex

Which figures are convex and which are concave?

  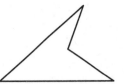 

24 25 26 27

_____ _____ _____ _____

© Houghton Mifflin Harcourt Publishing Company

Name Polygons

VOCABULARY
pentagon   hexagon
octagon   decagon

Polygons are named according to how many sides they have.

3 sides—**tri**angle   4 sides—**quad**rilateral   5 sides—**penta**gon

6 sides—**hexa**gon   8 sides—**octa**gon   10 sides—**deca**gon

Name each figure.

28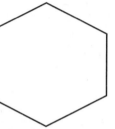

_____

29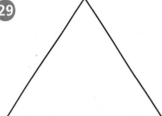

_____

30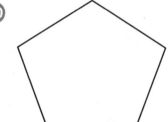

_____

31

_____

32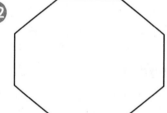

_____

33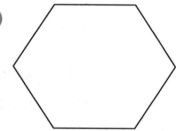

_____

34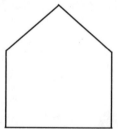

_____

35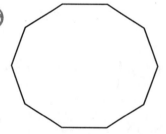

_____

36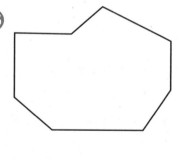

_____

✓ Check Understanding

Draw and describe three different triangles.

Triangles

Build Polygons from Triangles

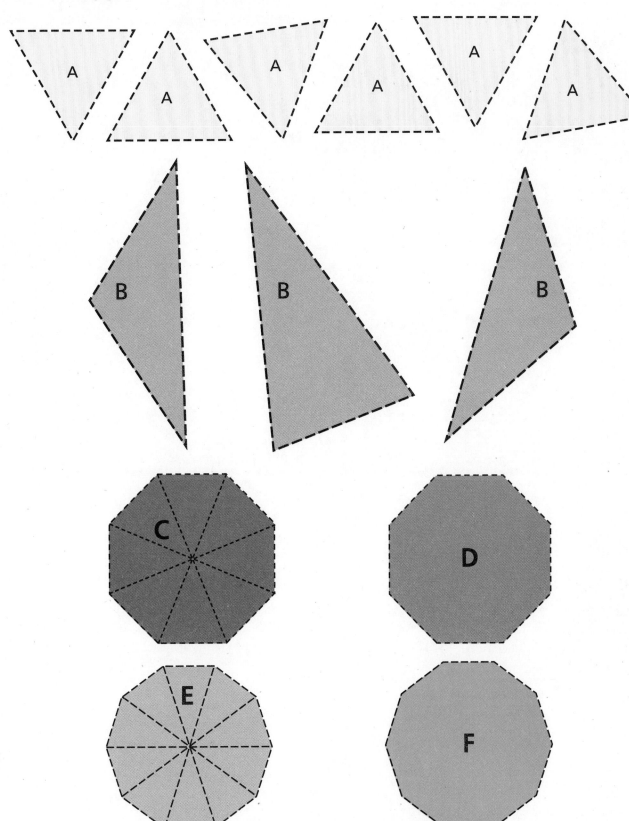

Triangles **427A**

Triangles

Describe Parallelograms

All of these figures are **parallelograms**.

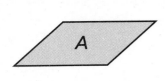 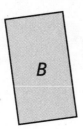  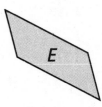

These figures are not parallelograms.

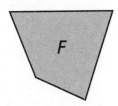 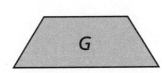   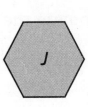

Complete the sentence.

1 A parallelogram is a quadrilateral with _____

_____

Measure Sides of Parallelograms

For each parallelogram, measure the sides to the nearest centimeter and label them with their lengths.

2    3 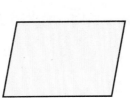   4

5 Look at the lengths of the sides. What patterns do

you notice? _____

Describe Rectangles

All of these figures are **rectangles**.

VOCABULARY
rectangle
square
rhombus

Adel said, "Rectangles are special kinds of parallelograms."

Complete the sentence.

6 A rectangle is a parallelogram with _____

_____

Explore Squares and Rhombuses

These figures are **squares**.   These figures are **rhombuses**.

Takeshi said, "Squares are special kinds of rectangles."

Cora said, "Rhombuses are special kinds of parallelograms."

Complete the sentence.

7 A square is a rectangle with _____

_____

8 A rhombus is a parallelogram with _____

_____

Parallelograms, Rectangles, Squares, and Rhombuses

Describe Quadrilaterals

Use as many words below as possible to describe each figure.

| quadrilateral | parallelogram | rectangle | square |

9 _____

10 _____

11 _____

12 _____

Describe Trapezoids

VOCABULARY
trapezoid
opposite sides

The quadrilaterals below are **trapezoids**.

 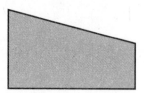 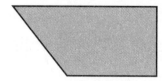

⑬ Write what you know about the **opposite sides** of a trapezoid.

_____

_____

⑭ Circle the quadrilaterals that are trapezoids.

 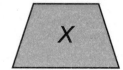 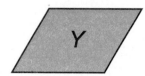 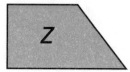

⑮ Explain why the figures you did not circle are not trapezoids.

_____

_____

_____

✓ **Check Understanding**
Draw a quadrilateral and describe it.

Parallelograms, Rectangles, Squares, and Rhombuses

Name _____

Draw Parallelograms

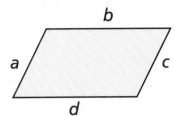

b

a c

d

1 Write what you know about the opposite sides
of a parallelogram.

_____

_____

2 Draw three different parallelograms.

CC SS Content Standards **3.G.A.1**
Mathematical Practices **MP5, MP7**

Draw Rectangles

VOCABULARY
adjacent sides

3 Write everything you know about the opposite sides of a rectangle.

_____

4 What do you know about the **adjacent sides** of a rectangle?

_____

5 Draw three different rectangles.

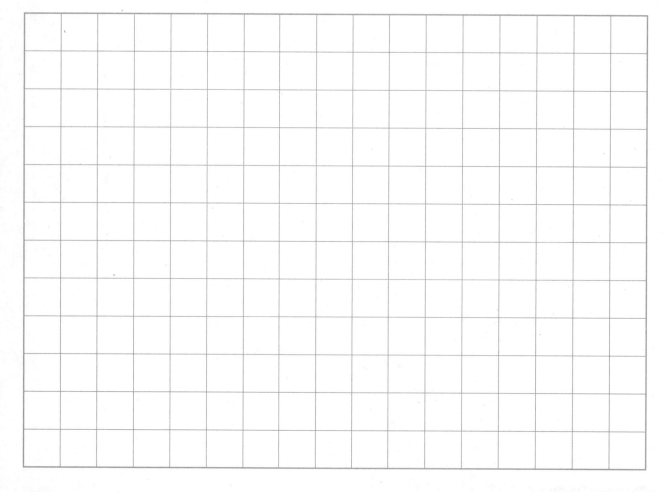

Draw Quadrilaterals

Draw Squares and Rhombuses

6 Write everything you know about squares.

_____

7 Write all you know about rhombuses.

_____

_____

8 Draw two different squares and two different rhombuses.

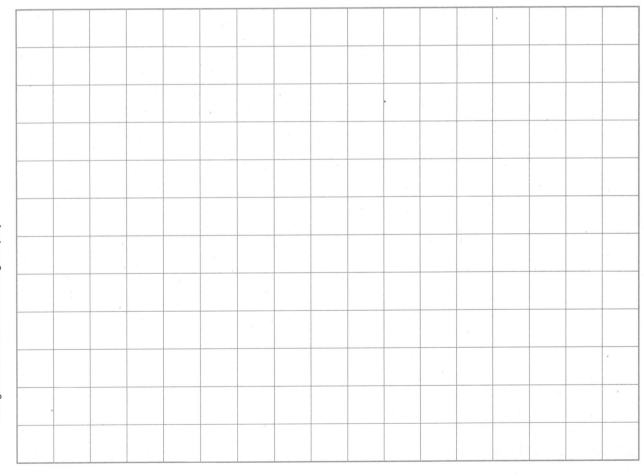

Draw Quadrilaterals That Are Not Squares, Rectangles, or Rhombuses

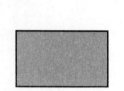   

9 What is a quadrilateral?

_____

10 Name all the quadrilaterals that have at least one pair of parallel sides.

_____

11 Draw three different quadrilaterals that are not squares, rectangles, or rhombuses.

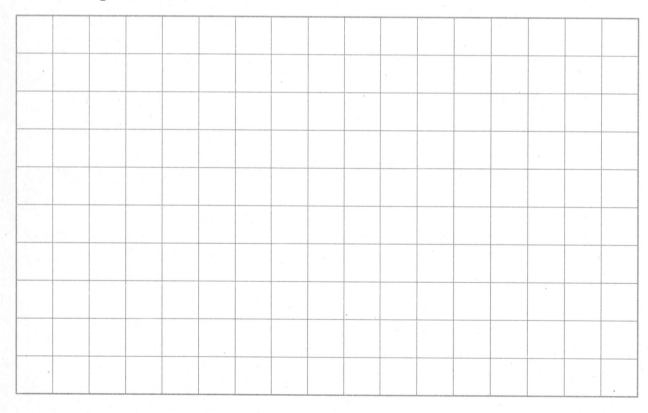

 Check Understanding

Draw a quadrilateral that is not a parallelogram.

Draw Quadrilaterals

Name _____

Name Quadrilaterals

Place a check mark beside every name that describes the figure.

1

☐ quadrilateral
☐ parallelogram
☐ rhombus
☐ rectangle
☐ square

2

☐ quadrilateral
☐ parallelogram
☐ rhombus
☐ rectangle
☐ trapezoid

3

☐ quadrilateral
☐ parallelogram
☐ rhombus
☐ rectangle
☐ square

4

☐ quadrilateral
☐ parallelogram
☐ rhombus
☐ rectangle
☐ square

5

☐ quadrilateral
☐ parallelogram
☐ rhombus
☐ rectangle
☐ square

6

☐ quadrilateral
☐ parallelogram
☐ rhombus
☐ rectangle
☐ square

7

☐ quadrilateral
☐ parallelogram
☐ rhombus
☐ rectangle
☐ square

8

☐ quadrilateral
☐ parallelogram
☐ rhombus
☐ rectangle
☐ square

9

☐ quadrilateral
☐ parallelogram
☐ rhombus
☐ rectangle
☐ square

Analyze Quadrilaterals

10 For each figure, put Xs under the descriptions that are always true.

	Four sides	Both pairs of opposite sides parallel	Both pairs of opposite sides the same length	Four right angles	All sides the same length
Quadrilateral					
Trapezoid					
Parallelogram					
Rhombus					
Rectangle					
Square					

Use the finished chart above to complete each statement.

11 Parallelograms have all the features of quadrilaterals *plus*

_____

_____

12 Rectangles have all the features of parallelograms *plus*

_____

13 Squares have all the features of quadrilaterals *plus*

_____

_____

14 Rhombuses have all the features of quadrilaterals *plus*

_____

_____

Classify Quadrilaterals

Name _____

Draw Quadrilaterals from a Description

Draw each figure.

15 Draw a quadrilateral that is *not* a parallelogram.

16 Draw a parallelogram that is *not* a rectangle.

17 Draw a rectangle that is *not* a square.

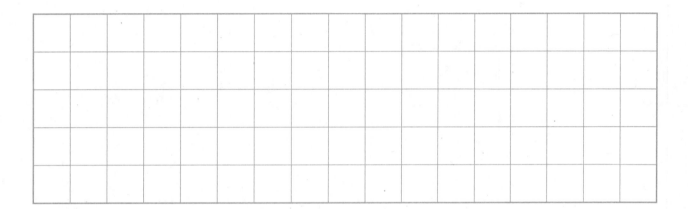

What's the Error?

Dear Math Students,

Today I had to draw a quadrilateral with parallel sides that is not a rectangle, square, or rhombus. This is my drawing.

Is my drawing correct? If not, please help me understand why it is wrong.

Your friend,
Puzzled Penguin

18 Write an answer to Puzzled Penguin.

_____

_____

Classify Quadrilaterals **437**

Sort and Classify Quadrilaterals

Use the category diagram to sort the figures you cut
out from Student Activity Book page 439A. Write the letter
of the figure in the diagram to record your work.

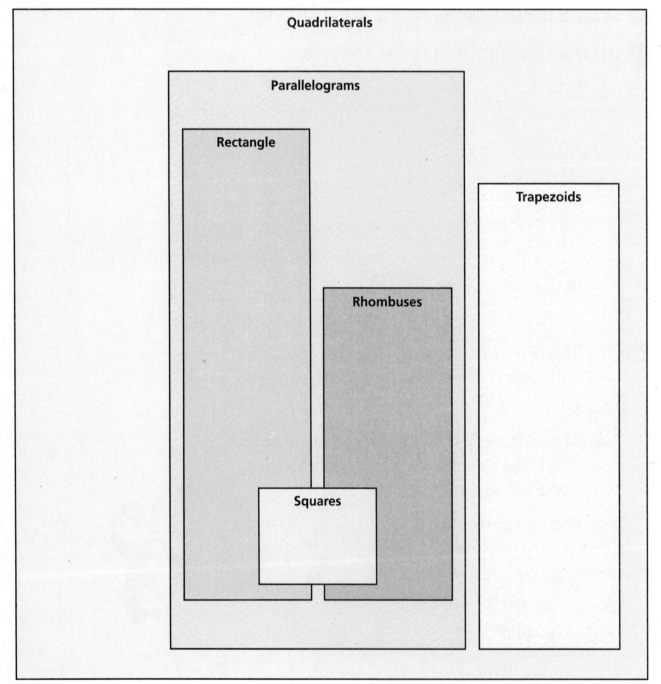

Quadrilaterals

Parallelograms

Rectangle

Trapezoids

Rhombuses

Squares

✓ Check Understanding

Complete the sentence. A rhombus is also a _____

and a _____.

Classify Quadrilaterals

Name _____

Quadrilaterals for Sorting

Cut along the dashed lines.

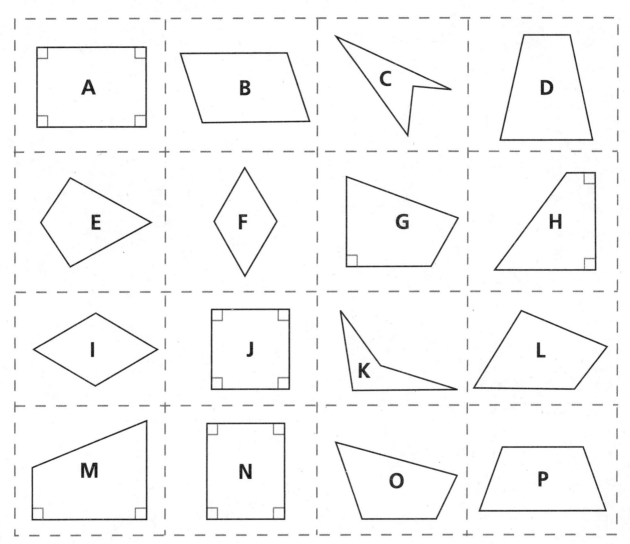

Classify Quadrilaterals

Name_____

Area and Gardening

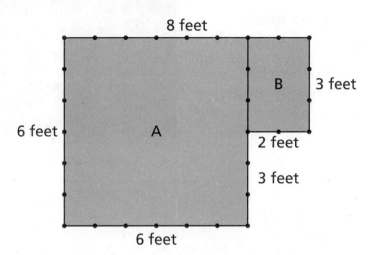

8 feet

B 3 feet

6 feet   A

2 feet

3 feet

6 feet

Look at the drawing of Yoakim's garden.
It is divided into two quadrilaterals.

1 What is the perimeter of part A? _____

What is the perimeter of part B? _____

2 What is the perimeter of the combined

garden? _____

3 Will Yoakim need more fencing to enclose the two
parts of his garden separately or to enclose the
combined garden? _____

_____

4 What is the area of part A? _____

What is the area of part B? _____

5 What is the area of the combined garden?

_____

6 How does the total area of the two parts of the garden
compare with the area of the combined garden?

_____

© Houghton Mifflin Harcourt Publishing Company

Design a Garden

Use the dot paper below to draw a different garden that has the same perimeter as Yoakim's combined garden. Beside it, draw a different garden that has the same area as Yoakim's garden.

|1 ft|

7 What is the area of your garden that has the same perimeter as Yoakim's garden?

_____

8 What is the perimeter of your garden that has the same area as Yoakim's garden?

_____

9 Use the centimeter dot paper at the right to draw separate areas within a garden where you would plant corn, beans, and tomatoes.

The area for corn is 12 square feet.
The area for beans is 25 square feet.
The area for tomatoes is 20 square feet.

Focus on Mathematical Practices

Write the correct answer.

1 What do a rhombus and a square have in common?

_____

2 Put a check mark beside every name
   that describes the figure.

☐ quadrilateral   ☐ rhombus

☐ not a quadrilateral   ☐ trapezoid

☐ rectangle   ☐ square

3 Which triangle has
   a right angle?

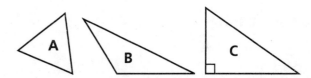

_____

4 List the figures that
   are quadrilaterals.

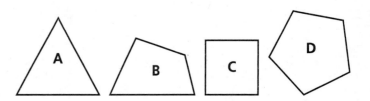

_____

5 List the figures that
   are quadrilaterals.

_____

Name _____   Date _____

Multiply or divide.

1 $2 \times 4 = \boxed{}$ **2** $9 \div 3 = \boxed{}$ **3** $6 \times 6 = \boxed{}$

4 $30 \div 6 = \boxed{}$ **5** $6 \times 9 = \boxed{}$ **6** $48 \div 8 = \boxed{}$

7 $4 \times 9 = \boxed{}$ **8** $72 \div 9 = \boxed{}$ **9** $8 \times 7 = \boxed{}$

Add or subtract.

10
$$\begin{array}{r} 563 \\ -\ 240 \\ \hline \end{array}$$

11
$$\begin{array}{r} 300 \\ +\ 620 \\ \hline \end{array}$$

12
$$\begin{array}{r} 562 \\ -\ 428 \\ \hline \end{array}$$

13
$$\begin{array}{r} 529 \\ +\ 386 \\ \hline \end{array}$$

14
$$\begin{array}{r} 338 \\ -\ 189 \\ \hline \end{array}$$

15
$$\begin{array}{r} 482 \\ +\ 379 \\ \hline \end{array}$$

1 Write the letter for each shape in the box that describes the shape.

 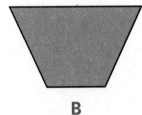 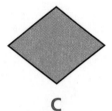 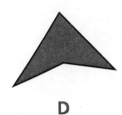

A   B   C   D

Quadrilateral	Parallelogram	Four right angles	All sides the same length

2 Draw two different parallelograms that are not squares or rhombuses.

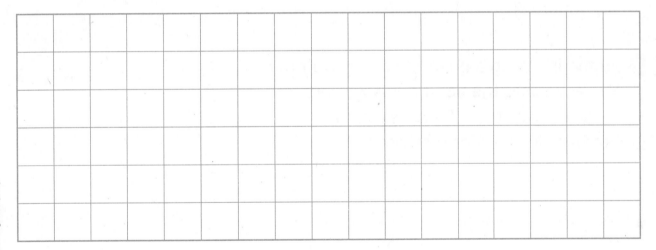

How did you decide which figures to draw?

3 Emily draws this figure.

For Exercises 3a–3e, choose Yes or No to tell whether the name describes the figure.

3a. quadrilateral   ○ Yes   ○ No

3b. rectangle   ○ Yes   ○ No

3c. parallelogram   ○ Yes   ○ No

3d. rhombus   ○ Yes   ○ No

3e. square   ○ Yes   ○ No

4 Emma is eating a bowl of soup for dinner. She estimates the bowl holds 2 quarts of soup. Do you think Emma's estimate is reasonable? Why or why not?

5 Matt's beach bucket contains 250 grams of sand.
He adds 130 grams of sand to the bucket. How
many grams of sand are in the bucket now?

_____ grams

6 Write the name of the object in the box that
shows the unit you would use to measure
the mass of the object.

| loaf of bread | watermelon | person |
| house key | lion | comb |

gram	kilogram

7 Estimate the liquid volume of each object.
Draw a line from the estimate to the object.

100 liters   3 liters   300 milliliters

8 Billy needs 200 milliliters of lemonade to fill
   a small jar. How many milliliters of lemonade
   does he need to fill 6 jars of the same size?

   Choose the measure to complete the sentence.

   Billy needs | 600 | milliliters of lemonade.
               | 800 |
               | 1,200 |

9 Draw a quadrilateral that is both a square and
   a rhombus.

   Is every rhombus also a square? Explain.

10 Mia uses 40 liters of water for her garden.
    That is 12 more liters than Rob. How many
    liters of water does Rob use?

    _____ liters

11 Rani uses a container that can hold 2 liters of water to fill a fish tank. The fish tank can hold 8 liters of water. How many times must she fill the smaller container to fill the fish tank?

_____ times

12 Sam uses 28 grams of chopped onions in his sauce. There are 6 grams of onions left. How many grams of onions did Sam start with?

_____ grams

13 Mei has 80 kilograms of firewood to divide equally into 10 bundles. How many kilograms of firewood should be in each bundle?

_____ kilograms

14 Chaseedah thinks this shape is a square. Anaya thinks the shape is a rectangle.

Who is correct? Explain your answer.

15 Roy uses 6 grams of corn in each veggie burger. How many grams of corn does he need to make 20 veggie burgers?

_____ grams

16 Janie has three dogs. The dogs have masses of 4 kilograms, 8 kilograms, and 7 kilograms. What is the total mass of the three dogs?

_____ kilograms

17 If each bag contains 185 grams of apple chips, how many grams of apple chips are in 3 bags?

_____ grams

18 Select all the figures that are quadrilaterals.

○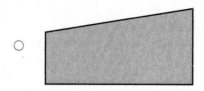

○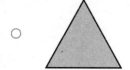

○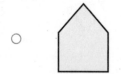

○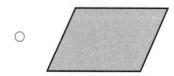

○

Can You Cut It?

Lucia's class is making sandwiches for a math fair. Lucia will cut the sandwiches into these three different shapes.

Shape A: a quadrilateral that is not a square

Shape B: a triangle with one right angle

Shape C: a parallelogram that is not a rectangle

1 Use your ruler to help you draw Lucia's shapes.

2 Label the shapes **Shape A, Shape B,** and **Shape C.**

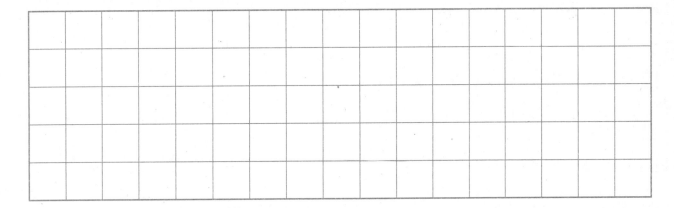

3 Combine 2 or more of your shapes to create a different quadrilateral.

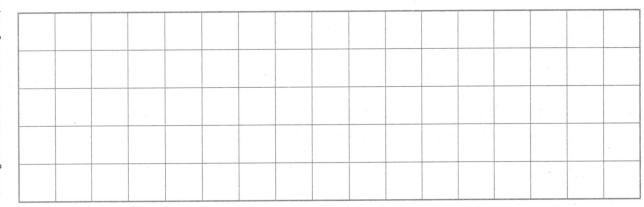

4 Lucia's class wants to serve a salad with the
sandwiches. Each salad will contain 30 grams of
chopped lettuce. How many grams of lettuce is
needed for 8 salads?

5 Each salad also contains 20 grams of tomatoes,
20 grams of cucumbers, and 20 grams of spinach.
What is the mass in grams of one salad?

6 What is the mass in grams of 8 salads?

7 The mass of a club sandwich is 269 grams. What
is the combined mass of one salad and one club
sandwich?

8 Mr. Juarez buys 2 club sandwiches and 1 salad.
What is the combined mass of the items he buys?

Halves and Fourths in Measurement

Fractions in Measurement

Halves	Quarters

Length

Money

Half-Dollar   Half-Dollar

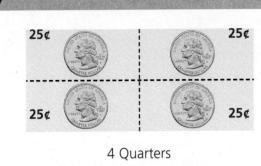

4 Quarters

Time

30 minutes + 30 minutes
= 60 minutes
= 1 hour

15 minutes + 15 minutes +
15 minutes + 15 minutes
= 60 minutes
= 1 hour

Liquid Capacity

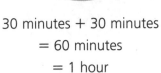

© Houghton Mifflin Harcourt Publishing Company

Measures and Units of Time

Table of Measures

Metric	Customary

Length/Area

Metric	Customary
1 meter (m) = 10 decimeters (dm) 1 meter (m) = 100 centimeters (cm) 1 decimeter (dm) = 10 centimeters (cm) 1 square centimeter = 1 cm² A metric unit for measuring area. It is the area of a square that is one centimeter on each side.	1 foot (ft) = 12 inches (in.) 1 yard = 3 feet (ft) 1 mile (mi) = 5,280 feet (ft) 1 square inch = 1 in² A customary unit for measuring area. It is the area of a square that is one inch on each side.

Liquid Volume

Metric	Customary
1 liter (L) = 1,000 milliliters (mL)	1 tablespoon (tbsp) = $\frac{1}{2}$ fluid ounce (fl oz) 1 cup (c) = 8 fluid ounces (fl oz) 1 pint (pt) = 2 cups (c) 1 quart (qt) = 2 pints (pt) 1 gallon (gal) = 4 quarts (qt)

Table of Units of Time

Time

1 minute (min) = 60 seconds (sec) 1 hour (hr) = 60 minutes 1 day = 24 hours 1 week (wk) = 7 days 1 month, about 30 days 1 year (yr) = 12 months (mo) or about 52 weeks	1 year = 365 days 1 leap year = 366 days

© Houghton Mifflin Harcourt Publishing Company

Properties of Operations

Associative Property of Addition

$(a + b) + c = a + (b + c)$	$(2 + 5) + 3 = 2 + (5 + 3)$

Commutative Property of Addition

$a + b = b + a$	$4 + 6 = 6 + 4$

Identity Property of Addition

$a + 0 = 0 + a = a$	$3 + 0 = 0 + 3 = 3$

Associative Property of Multiplication

$(a \cdot b) \cdot c = a \cdot (b \cdot c)$	$(3 \cdot 5) \cdot 7 = 3 \cdot (5 \cdot 7)$

Commutative Property of Multiplication

$a \cdot b = b \cdot a$	$6 \cdot 3 = 3 \cdot 6$

Identity Property of Multiplication

$a \cdot 1 = 1 \cdot a = a$	$8 \cdot 1 = 1 \cdot 8 = 8$

Zero Property of Multiplication

$a \cdot 0 = 0 \cdot a = 0$	$5 \cdot 0 = 0 \cdot 5 = 0$

Distributive Property of Multiplication over Addition

$a \cdot (b + c) = (a \cdot b) + (a \cdot c)$	$2 \cdot (4 + 3) = (2 \cdot 4) + (2 \cdot 3)$

Problem Types

Addition and Subtraction Problem Types

	Result Unknown	Change Unknown	Start Unknown
Add to	Aisha had 274 stamps in her collection. Then her grandfather gave her 65 stamps. How many stamps does she have now? *Situation and solution equation:*[1] $274 + 65 = s$	Aisha had 274 stamps in her collection. Then her grandfather gave her some stamps. Now she has 339 stamps. How many stamps did her grandfather give her? *Situation equation:* $274 + s = 339$ *Solution equation:* $s = 339 - 274$	Aisha had some stamps in her collection. Then her grandfather gave her 65 stamps. Now she has 339 stamps. How many stamps did she have to start? *Situation equation* $s + 65 = 339$ *Solution equation:* $s = 339 - 65$
Take from	A store had 750 bottles of water at the start of the day. During the day, the store sold 490 bottles. How many bottles did they have at the end of the day? *Situation and solution equation:* $750 - 490 = b$	A store had 750 bottles of water at the start of the day. The store had 260 bottles left at the end of the day. How many bottles did the store sell? *Situation equation:* $750 - b = 260$ *Solution equation:* $b = 750 - 260$	A store had a number of bottles of water at the start of the day. The store sold 490 bottles of water. At the end of the day 260 bottles were left. How many bottles did the store have to start with? *Situation equation:* $b - 490 = 260$ *Solution equation:* $b = 260 + 490$

[1]A situation equation represents the structure (action) in the problem situation. A solution equation shows the operation used to find the answer.

Addition and Subtraction Problem Types

	Total Unknown	Addend Unknown	Other Addend Unknown
Put Together/ Take Apart	A clothing store has 375 shirts with short sleeves and 148 shirts with long sleeves. How many shirts does the store have in all? *Math drawing:* s over 375 and 148 *Situation and solution equation:* $375 + 148 = s$	Of the 523 shirts in a clothing store, 375 have short sleeves. The rest have long sleeves. How many shirts have long sleeves? *Math drawing:* 523 over 375 and s *Situation equation:* $523 = 375 + s$ *Solution equation:* $s = 523 - 375$	A clothing store has 523 shirts. Some have short sleeves and 148 have long sleeves. How many of the shirts have short sleeves? *Math drawing:* 523 over s and 148 *Situation equation* $523 = s + 148$ *Solution equation:* $s = 523 - 148$

Addition and Subtraction Problem Types (continued)

	Difference Unknown	Greater Unknown	Smaller Unknown
Compare	At a zoo, the female black bear weighs 175 pounds. The male black bear weighs 260 pounds. How much more does the male black bear weigh than the female black bear? At a zoo, the female black bear weighs 175 pounds. The male black bear weighs 260 pounds. How much less does the female black bear weigh than the male black bear? *Math drawing:* 260 175 d *Situation equation:* $175 + d = 260$ or $d = 260 - 175$ *Solution equation:* $d = 260 - 175$	**Leading Language** At a zoo, the female black bear weighs 175 pounds. The male black bear weighs 85 pounds more than the female black bear. How much does the male black bear weigh? **Misleading Language** At a zoo, the female black bear weighs 175 pounds. The female black bear weighs 85 pounds less than the male black bear. How much does the male black bear weigh? *Math drawing:* m 175 85 *Situation and solution equation:* $175 + 85 = m$	**Leading Language** At a zoo, the male black bear weighs 260 pounds. The female black bear weighs 85 pounds less than the male black bear. How much does the female black bear weigh? **Misleading Language** At a zoo, the male black bear weighs 260 pounds. The male black bear weighs 85 pounds more than the female black bear. How much does the female black bear weigh? *Math drawing:* 260 f 85 *Situation equation* $f + 85 = 260$ or $f = 260 - 85$ *Solution equation:* $f = 260 - 85$

A comparison sentence can always be said in two ways. One way uses *more*, and the other uses *fewer* or *less*. Misleading language suggests the wrong operation. For example, it says *the female black bear weighs 85 pounds less than the male*, but you have to add 85 pounds to the female's weight to get the male's weight.

Multiplication and Division Problem Types

	Unknown Product	Group Size Unknown	Number of Groups Unknown
Equal Groups	A teacher bought 5 boxes of markers. There are 8 markers in each box. How many markers did the teacher buy? Math drawing: *Situation and solution equation:* $n = 5 \cdot 8$	A teacher bought 5 boxes of markers. She bought 40 markers in all. How many markers are in each box? Math drawing: *Situation equation:* $5 \cdot n = 40$ *Solution equation:* $n = 40 \div 5$	A teacher bought boxes of 8 markers. She bought 40 markers in all. How many boxes of markers did she buy? Math drawing: *Situation equation* $n \cdot 8 = 40$ *Solution equation:* $n = 40 \div 8$

Problem Types

Multiplication and Division Problem Types (continued)

	Unknown Product	Unknown Factor	Unknown Factor
Arrays	For the yearbook photo, the drama club stood in 3 rows of 7 students. How many students were in the photo in all? Math drawing: $\begin{matrix}&7\\3&\circ\circ\circ\circ\circ\circ\circ\\&\circ\circ\circ\circ\circ\circ\circ\\&\circ\circ\circ\circ\circ\circ\circ\end{matrix}$ Situation and solution equation: $n = 3 \cdot 7$	For the yearbook photo, the 21 students in drama club stood in 3 equal rows. How many students were in each row? Math drawing: n n → Total: 21 n Situation equation: $3 \cdot n = 21$ Solution equation: $n = 21 \div 3$	For the yearbook photo, the 21 students in drama club stood in rows of 7 students. How many rows were there? Math drawing: 7 7 → Total: 21 7 Situation equation $n \cdot 7 = 21$ Solution equation: $n = 21 \div 7$
Area	The floor of the kitchen is 2 meters by 5 meters. What is the area of the floor? Math drawing: $\begin{array}{c}5\\2\,[\;A\;]\end{array}$ Situation and solution equation: $A = 5 \cdot 2$	The floor of the kitchen is 5 meters long. The area of the floor is 10 square meters. What is the width of the floor? Math drawing: $\begin{array}{c}5\\w\,[\;10\;]\end{array}$ Situation equation: $5 \cdot w = 10$ Solution equation: $w = 10 \div 5$	The floor of the kitchen is 2 meters wide. The area of the floor is 10 square meters. What is the length of the floor? Math drawing: $\begin{array}{c}l\\2\,[\;10\;]\end{array}$ Situation equation $l \cdot 2 = 10$ Solution equation: $l = 10 \div 2$

MathWord **Power**

Word Review

Work with a partner. Choose a word from a current unit or a review word from a previous unit. Use the word to complete one of the activities listed on the right. Then ask your partner if they have any edits to your work or questions about what you described. Repeat, having your partner choose a word.

Activities

- Give the meaning in words or gestures.
- Use the word in the sentence.
- Give another word that is related to the word in some way and explain the relationship.

Crossword Puzzle

Create a crossword puzzle similar to the example below. Use vocabulary words from the unit. You can add other related words, too. Challenge your partner to solve the puzzle.

				⁴s	u	m	
	¹a			u			
	d			b			
¹a	d	d	i	t	i	o	³n
	e			r			u
	n			a			m
²a	d	d		c			b
				t			e
				i			r
³r	e	g	r	o	u	p	
				n			

Across
1. _____ and subtraction are inverse operations.
2. To put amounts together
3. When you trade 10 ones for 1 ten, you _____.
4. The answer to an addition problem

Down
1. In $24 + 65 = 89$, 24 is an _____.
2. A combination of the digits 0, 1, 2, 3, 4, 5, 6, 7, 8, and 9
3. The operation that you can use to find out how much more one number is than another

Vocabulary Activities

Word Wall

With your teacher's permission, start a word wall in your classroom. As you work through each lesson, put the math vocabulary words on index cards and place them on the word wall. You can work with a partner or a small group choosing a word and giving the definition.

Word Web

Make a word web for a word or words you do not understand in a unit. Fill in the web with words or phrases that are related to the vocabulary word.

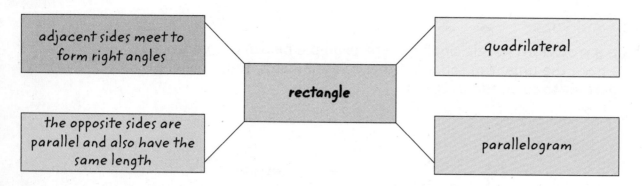

Alphabet Challenge

Take an alphabet challenge. Choose three letters from the alphabet. Think of three vocabulary words for each letter. Then write the definition or draw an example for each word.

A	D	L
addition	data	liter
array	denominator	line segment
area	divide	line plot

Concentration

Write the vocabulary words and related words from a unit on index cards. Write the definitions on a different set of index cards. Mix up both sets of cards. Then place the cards facedown on a table in an array, for example, 3 by 3 or 3 by 4. Take turns turning over two cards. If one card is a word and one card is a definition that matches the word, take the pair. Continue until each word has been matched with its definition.

area

the number of square units in a region

Math Journal

As you learn new words, write them in your Math Journal. Write the definition of the word and include a sketch or an example. As you learn new information about the word, add notes to your definition.

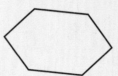

polygon: a closed plane figure with sides made of straight line segments.

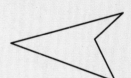

In concave polygons, there exists a line segment with endpoints inside the polygon and a point on the line segment that is outside the polygon.

What's the Word?

Work together to make a poster or bulletin board display of the words in a unit. Write definitions on a set of index cards. Mix up the cards. Work with a partner, choosing a definition from the index cards. Have your partner point to the word on the poster and name the matching math vocabulary word. Switch roles and try the activity again.

the bottom number in a fraction that shows the total number of equal parts in the whole

fraction	fourths
unit fraction	eighths
denominator	halves
numerator	sixths
equivalent	
equivalent fractions	
equivalence chain	
thirds	

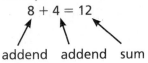

addend
One of two or more numbers to be added together to find a sum.

Example:

$$8 + 4 = 12$$

addend   addend   sum

addition
A mathematical operation that combines two or more numbers.

Example:

$$23 + 52 = 75$$

addend   addend   sum

adjacent sides
Two sides of a figure that meet at a point.

Example:
Sides a and b are adjacent.

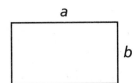

A.M.
The time period between midnight and noon.

analog clock
A clock with a face and hands.

angle
A figure formed by two rays or two line segments that meet at an endpoint.

area
The total number of square units that cover a figure.

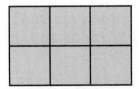

Example:
The area of the rectangle is 6 square units.

array
An arrangement of objects, pictures, or numbers in columns and rows.

Associative Property of Addition (Grouping Property of Addition)
The property stating that changing the way in which addends are grouped does not change the sum.

Example:
$$(2 + 3) + 1 = 2 + (3 + 1)$$
$$5 + 1 = 2 + 4$$
$$6 = 6$$

Glossary

Associative Property of Multiplication (Grouping Property of Multiplication)

The property stating that changing the way in which factors are grouped does not change the product.

Example:

$(2 \times 3) \times 4 = 2 \times (3 \times 4)$

$6 \times 4 = 2 \times 12$

$24 = 24$

axis (plural: axes)

A reference line for a graph. A graph has 2 axes; one is horizontal and the other is vertical.

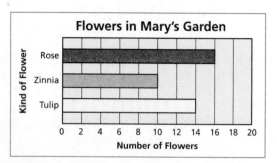

B

bar graph

A graph that uses bars to show data. The bars may be horizontal, as in the graph above, or vertical, as in the graph below.

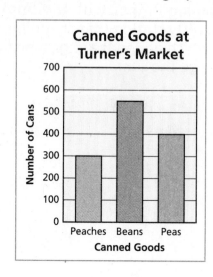

C

capacity

The amount a container can hold.

centimeter (cm)

A metric unit used to measure length.

100 centimeters = 1 meter

column

A part of a table or array that contains items arranged vertically.

Commutative Property of Addition (Order Property of Addition)

The property stating that changing the order of addends does not change the sum.

Example:

$3 + 7 = 7 + 3$

$10 = 10$

Commutative Property of Multiplication (Order Property of Multiplication)

The property stating that changing the order of factors does not change the product.

Example:

$5 \times 4 = 4 \times 5$

$20 = 20$

comparison bars*

Bars that represent the greater amount, lesser amount, and difference in a comparison problem.

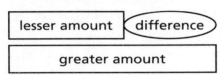

concave

A polygon for which you can connect two points inside the polygon with a segment that passes outside the polygon.

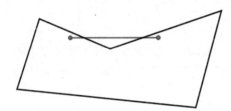

convex

A polygon is convex if all of its diagonals are inside it.

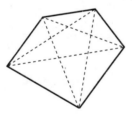

cup (c)

A customary unit of measure used to measure capacity.

1 cup = 8 fluid ounces

2 cups = 1 pint

4 cups = 1 quart

16 cups = 1 gallon

D

data

Pieces of information.

decagon

A polygon with 10 sides.

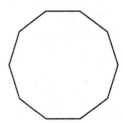

decimeter (dm)

A metric unit used to measure length.

1 decimeter = 10 centimeters

decompose

To separate or break apart (a geometric figure or a number) into smaller parts.

denominator

The bottom number in a fraction, which shows the total number of equal parts in the whole.

Example:

$\frac{1}{3}$ ◄——— denominator

diagonal

A line segment that connects two corners of a figure and is not a side of the figure.

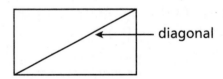

difference

The result of subtraction or of comparing.

digit

Any of the symbols 0, 1, 2, 3, 4, 5, 6, 7, 8, 9.

*A classroom research-based term developed for *Math Expressions*

Glossary

digital clock
A clock that displays the hour and minutes with numbers.

Distributive Property
You can multiply a sum by a number, or multiply each addend by the number and add the products; the result is the same.

Example:
$3 \times (2 + 4) = (3 \times 2) + (3 \times 4)$

| 3×6 | $=$ | 6 | $+$ | 12 |
| | 18 | $=$ | | 18 |

dividend
The number that is divided in division.

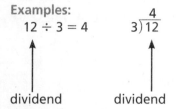

Examples:
$12 \div 3 = 4$ $3\overline{)12}$ with 4 above

dividend   dividend

division
The mathematical operation that separates an amount into smaller equal groups to find the number of groups or the number in each group.

Example:
$12 \div 3 = 4$ is a division number sentence.

divisor
The number that you divide by in division.

Example: 4
$12 \div 3 = 4$ $3\overline{)12}$

divisor   divisor

E

elapsed time
The time that passes between the beginning and the end of an activity.

endpoint
The point at either end of a line segment or the beginning point of a ray.

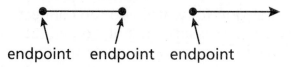

endpoint   endpoint   endpoint

equal groups
Two or more groups with the same number of items in each group.

equation
A mathematical sentence with an equal sign.

Examples:
$11 + 22 = 33$
$75 - 25 = 50$

equivalent
Equal, or naming the same amount.

equivalent fractions
Fractions that name the same amount.

Example:
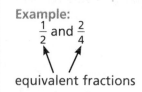
$\frac{1}{2}$ and $\frac{2}{4}$

equivalent fractions

estimate
A reasonable guess about how many or about how much.

even number
A whole number that is a multiple of 2. The ones digit in an even number is 0, 2, 4, 6, or 8.

expanded form
A number written to show the value of each of its digits.

Examples:
347 = 300 + 40 + 7
347 = 3 hundreds + 4 tens + 7 ones

expression
A combination of numbers, variables, and/or operation signs. An expression does not have an equal sign.

Examples:
4 + 7   a − 3

F

factor
Any of the numbers that are multiplied to give a product.

Example:
4 × 5 = 20

factor   factor   product

fluid ounce (fl oz)
A unit of liquid volume in the customary system that equals $\frac{1}{8}$ cup or 2 tablespoons.

foot (ft)
A customary unit used to measure length.

1 foot = 12 inches

fraction
A number that names part of a whole or part of a set.

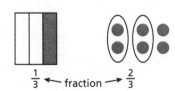

$\frac{1}{3}$ ← fraction → $\frac{2}{3}$

frequency table
A table that shows how many times each event, item, or category occurs.

Frequency Table	
Age	Tally
7	1
8	3
9	5
10	4
11	2

function table
A table of ordered pairs that shows a function.

For every input number, there is only one possible output number.

Rule: add 2	
Input	Output
1	3
2	4
3	5
4	6

G

gallon (gal)
A customary unit used to measure capacity.

1 gallon = 4 quarts = 8 pints = 16 cups

gram (g)
A metric unit of mass. One paper clip has a mass of about 1 gram.

1,000 grams = 1 kilogram

Glossary

greater than (>)
A symbol used to compare two numbers.

Example:
6 > 5

6 *is greater than* 5.

group
To combine numbers to form new tens, hundreds, thousands, and so on.

H

height
A vertical distance, or how tall something is.

hexagon
A polygon with six sides.

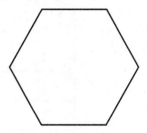

horizontal
Extending in two directions, left and right.

horizontal bar graph
A bar graph with horizontal bars.

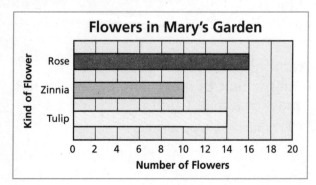

Flowers in Mary's Garden

hundreds

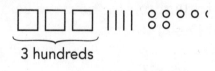

3 hundreds

347 has 3 hundreds.

↑

hundreds

I

Identity Property of Addition
If 0 is added to a number, the sum equals that number.

Example:
3 + 0 = 3

Identity Property of Multiplication
The product of 1 and any number equals that number.

Example:
10 × 1 = 10

improper fraction
A fraction in which the numerator is equal to or is greater than the denominator. Improper fractions are equal to or greater than 1.
$\frac{5}{5}$ and $\frac{8}{3}$ are improper fractions.

inch (in.)
A customary unit used to measure length.

12 inches = 1 foot

K

key
A part of a map, graph, or chart that explains what symbols mean.

kilogram (kg)
A metric unit of mass.
1 kilogram = 1,000 grams

kilometer (km)
A metric unit of length.
1 kilometer = 1,000 meters

L

less than (<)
A symbol used to compare numbers.

Example:
5 < 6
5 *is less than* 6.

line
A straight path that goes on forever in opposite directions.

line plot
A diagram that shows frequency of data on a number line. Also called a *dot plot*.

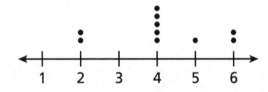

line segment
A part of a line. A line segment has two endpoints.

liquid volume
A measure of how much a container can hold. Also called *capacity*.

liter (L)
A metric unit used to measure capacity.
1 liter = 1,000 milliliters

M

mass
The amount of matter in an object.

mental math
A way to solve problems without using pencil and paper or a calculator.

meter (m)
A metric unit used to measure length.
1 meter = 100 centimeters

method
A procedure, or way, of doing something.

mile (mi)
A customary unit of length.
1 mile = 5,280 feet

milliliter (mL)
A metric unit used to measure capacity.
1,000 milliliters = 1 liter

mixed number
A whole number and a fraction.
$1\frac{3}{4}$ is a mixed number.

multiple
A number that is the product of the given number and any whole number.

multiplication
A mathematical operation that combines equal groups.

Example:

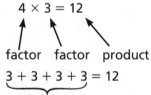

Glossary

N

number line
A line on which numbers are assigned to lengths.

numerator
The top number in a fraction that shows the number of equal parts counted.

Example:

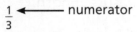

$\frac{1}{3}$ ◄———— numerator

O

octagon
A polygon with eight sides.

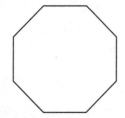

odd number
A whole number that is not a multiple of 2. The ones digit in an odd number is 1, 3, 5, 7, or 9.

ones

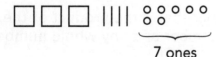

7 ones

347 has 7 ones.

ones

opposite sides
Sides of a polygon that are across from each other; they do not meet at a point.

Example:

Sides *a* and *c* are opposite.

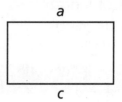

Order of Operations
A set of rules that state the order in which the operations in an expression should be done.

STEP 1: Perform operations inside parentheses first.

STEP 2: Multiply and divide from left to right.

STEP 3: Add and subtract from left to right.

ounce (oz)
A customary unit used to measure weight.

16 ounces = 1 pound

P

parallel lines
Two lines that are the same distance apart.

parallelogram
A quadrilateral with both pairs of opposite sides parallel.

pentagon
A polygon with five sides.

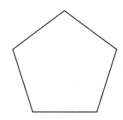

perimeter
The distance around a figure.

Example:
Perimeter = 3 cm + 5 cm + 3 cm + 5 cm = 16 cm

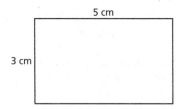

5 cm

3 cm

pictograph
A graph that uses pictures or symbols to represent data.

Favorite Ice Cream Flavors

Peanut Butter Crunch	🍦 🍦
Cherry Vanilla	🍦 🍦 🍦
Chocolate	🍦 🍦 🍦 🍦 🍦

Each 🍦 stands for 4 votes.

pint (pt)
A customary unit used to measure capacity.

1 pint = 2 cups

place value
The value assigned to the place that a digit occupies in a number.

9   6   2

hundreds tens ones

place value drawing
A drawing that represents a number. Hundreds are represented by boxes, tens by vertical lines, and ones by small circles.

962

P.M
The time period between noon and midnight.

polygon
A closed plane figure with sides made up of straight line segments.

pound (lb)
A customary unit used to measure weight.

1 pound = 16 ounces

product
The answer when you multiply numbers.

Example:

4 × 7 = 28

factor   factor   product

proof drawing*
A drawing used to show that an answer is correct.

```
  249
+ 386
  11
  635
```

*A classroom research-based term developed for *Math Expressions*

Glossary

Q

quadrilateral
A polygon with four sides.

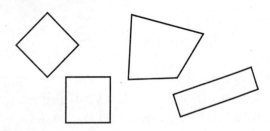

quart (qt)
A customary unit used to measure capacity.

1 quart = 4 cups

quotient
The answer when you divide numbers.

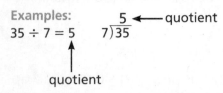

Examples:
$35 \div 7 = 5$ $\quad$ 7)$\overline{35}$ ← quotient

quotient

R

ray
A part of a line that has one endpoint and goes on forever in one direction.

rectangle
A parallelogram that has 4 right angles.

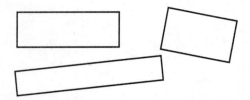

rhombus
A parallelogram with equal sides.

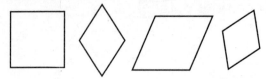

right angle
An angle that measures 90°.

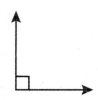

round
To find about how many or how much by expressing a number to the nearest ten, hundred, thousand, and so on.

row
A part of a table or array that contains items arranged horizontally.

S

scale
An arrangement of numbers in order with equal intervals.

side (of a figure)
One of the line segments that make up a polygon.

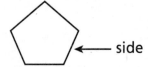

side

simplify
To write an equivalent fraction with a smaller numerator and denominator.

situation equation*
An equation that shows the action or the relationship in a problem.

Example:
$35 + n = 40$

solution equation*
An equation that shows the operation to perform in order to solve the problem.

Example:
$n = 40 - 35$

square
A rectangle with four sides of the same length.

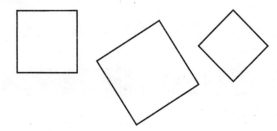

square number
The product of a whole number and itself.

Example:
$4 \times 4 = 16$

↑

square number

square unit
A unit of area equal to the area of a square with one-unit sides.

standard form
The name of a number written using digits.

Example:
1,829

subtract
To find the difference of two numbers.

Example:
$18 - 11 = 7$

subtraction
A mathematical operation on two numbers that gives the difference.

Example:
$43 - 40 = 3$

sum
The answer when adding two or more addends.

Example:
$37 + 52 = 89$

addend   addend   sum

T

table
An easy-to-read arrangement of data, usually in rows and columns.

Favorite Team Sport	
Sport	**Number of Students**
Baseball	35
Soccer	60
Basketball	40

*A classroom research-based term developed for *Math Expressions*

Glossary

tally chart
A chart used to record and organize data with tally marks.

Tally Chart

Age	Tally
7	I
8	III
9	⊬Ш

tally marks
Short line segments drawn in groups of 5. Each mark, including the slanted mark, stands for 1 unit.

 means 13
    5   5   3

tens

4 tens

347 has 4 tens.
↑
tens

total
The answer when adding two or more addends. The sum of two or more numbers.

Example:
$$672 + 228 = 900$$

addend   *addend*   total *sum*

trapezoid
A quadrilateral with exactly one pair of parallel sides.

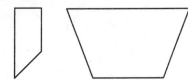

triangle
A polygon with three sides.

---

ungroup*
To open up 1 in a given place to make 10 of the next smaller place value in order to subtract.

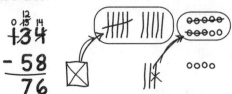

unit fraction
A fraction whose numerator is 1. It shows one equal part of a whole.

Example:

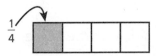
$\frac{1}{4}$

unit square
A square whose area is 1 square unit.

variable
A letter or symbol used to represent an unknown number in an algebraic expression or equation.

Example:
$2 + n$
n is a variable.

Venn diagram
A diagram that uses circles to show the relationship among sets of objects.

At least one pair   Exactly two sides
of parallel sides   of equal length

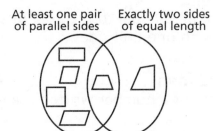

*A classroom research-based term developed for *Math Expressions*

© Houghton Mifflin Harcourt Publishing Company

vertex

A point where sides, rays, or edges meet.

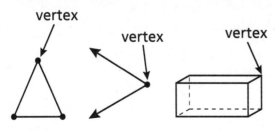

vertical

Extending in two directions, up and down.

vertical bar graph

A bar graph with vertical bars.

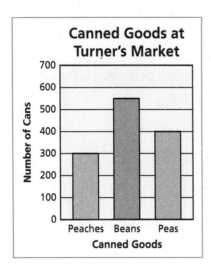

W

weight

The measure of how heavy something is.

word form

A name of a number written using words instead of digits.

Example:
Nine hundred eighty-four

Y

yard (yd)

A customary unit used to measure length.

1 yard = 3 feet = 36 inches

Z

Zero Property of Multiplication

If 0 is multiplied by a number, the product is 0.

Example:
$3 \times 0 = 0$

3.OA Operations and Algebraic Thinking

Represent and solve problems involving multiplication and division.

3.OA.A.1	Interpret products of whole numbers, e.g., interpret 5×7 as the total number of objects in 5 groups of 7 objects each.	Unit 1 Lessons 1, 2, 3, 4, 5, 6, 7, 8, 9, 10, 12, 13, 14, 16, 18, 19; Unit 2 Lessons 2, 4, 7, 9, 10, 11, 13, 15
3.OA.A.2	Interpret whole-number quotients of whole numbers, e.g., interpret $56 \div 8$ as the number of objects in each share when 56 objects are partitioned equally into 8 shares, or as a number of shares when 56 objects are partitioned into equal shares of 8 objects each.	Unit 1 Lessons 4, 5, 6, 7, 9, 10, 12, 13, 14, 15, 16, 17, 18, 19; Unit 2 Lessons 2, 4, 7, 9, 10, 11, 13, 15
3.OA.A.3	Use multiplication and division within 100 to solve word problems in situations involving equal groups, arrays, and measurement quantities, e.g., by using drawings and equations with a symbol for the unknown number to represent the problem.	Unit 1 Lessons 2, 3, 4, 5, 6, 7, 9, 10, 12, 13, 14, 16, 18, 19; Unit 2 Lessons 2, 4, 7, 9, 10, 11, 13, 15; Unit 4 Lesson 15; Unit 6 Lessons 2, 3, 7, 8, 9, 11; Unit 7 Lessons 1, 2, 3, 4
3.OA.A.4	Determine the unknown whole number in a multiplication or division equation relating three whole numbers.	Unit 1 Lessons 1, 4, 5, 6, 7, 8, 9, 10, 11, 12, 13, 14, 16, 18, 19; Unit 2 Lessons 1, 2, 3, 4, 5, 6, 7, 8, 9, 10, 11, 13, 14, 15; Unit 6 Lessons 2, 3

Understand properties of multiplication and the relationship between multiplication and division.

3.OA.B.5	Apply properties of operations as strategies to multiply and divide.	Unit 1 Lessons 3, 6, 11, 12, 14, 15, 19; Unit 2 Lessons 1, 8, 12, 15
3.OA.B.6	Understand division as an unknown-factor problem.	Unit 1 Lessons 4, 5, 6, 7, 8, 9, 10, 11, 12, 13, 14, 15, 16, 17, 18; Unit 2 Lessons 1, 2, 3, 4, 5, 6, 7, 8, 9, 10, 11, 12, 13, 14

Multiply and divide within 100.

3.OA.C.7	Fluently multiply and divide within 100, using strategies such as the relationship between multiplication and division or properties of operations. By the end of Grade 3, know from memory all products of two one-digit numbers.	Unit 1 Lessons 1, 2, 3, 4, 5, 6, 7, 8, 9, 10, 11, 12, 13, 14, 15, 16, 17, 18, 19; Unit 2 Lessons 1, 2, 3, 4, 5, 6, 7, 8, 9, 10, 11, 12, 13, 14, 15

■ **Major**	■ **Supporting**	■ **Additional**

Solve problems involving the four operations, and identify and explain patterns in arithmetic.

3.OA.D.8	Solve two-step word problems using the four operations. Represent these problems using equations with a letter standing for the unknown quantity. Assess the reasonableness of answers using mental computation and estimation strategies including rounding.	Unit 2 Lessons 9, 10, 11, 13; Unit 3 Lesson 17; Unit 6 Lessons 7, 8, 9, 10, 11
3.OA.D.9	Identify arithmetic patterns (including patterns in the addition table or multiplication table), and explain them using properties of operations.	Unit 1 Lessons 1, 5, 6, 7, 8, 10, 12, 15, 19; Unit 2 Lessons 1, 3, 5, 6, 8, 14, 15; Unit 3 Lessons 17

3.NBT Number and Operations in Base Ten

Use place value understanding and properties of operations to perform multi-digit arithmetic.

3.NBT.A.1	Use place value understanding to round whole numbers to the nearest 10 or 100.	Unit 3 Lessons 1, 2, 3, 4, 5, 6, 10, 17, 18; Unit 6 Lesson 4
3.NBT.A.2	Fluently add and subtract within 1000 using strategies and algorithms based on place value, properties of operations, and/or the relationship between addition and subtraction.	Unit 3 Lessons 1, 2, 3, 4, 5, 6, 7, 8, 9, 10, 11, 12, 13, 14, 15, 16, 17, 18; Unit 4 Lessons 12, 13; Unit 6 Lessons 1, 2, 3, 4, 5, 6, 7, 8, 9, 10, 11
3.NBT.A.3	Multiply one-digit whole numbers by multiples of 10 in the range 10–90 (e.g., 9 × 80, 5 × 60) using strategies based on place value and properties of operations.	Unit 2 Lesson 12

3.NF Number and Operations–Fractions

Develop understanding of fractions as numbers.

3.NF.A.1	Understand a fraction $\frac{1}{b}$ as the quantity formed by 1 part when a whole is partitioned into b equal parts; understand a fraction $\frac{a}{b}$ as the quantity formed by a parts of size $\frac{1}{b}$.	Unit 4 Lessons 1, 2 Unit 5 Lesson 10
3.NF.A.2	Understand a fraction as a number on the number line; represent fractions on a number line diagram.	Unit 4 Lessons 2, 3; Unit 5 Lesson 9
3.NF.A.2.a	Represent a fraction $\frac{1}{b}$ on a number line diagram by defining the interval from 0 to 1 as the whole and partitioning it into b equal parts. Recognize that each part has size $\frac{1}{b}$ and that the endpoint of the part based at 0 locates the number $\frac{1}{b}$ on the number line.	Unit 4 Lessons 2, 3; Unit 5 Lesson 9

3.NF.A.2.b	Represent a fraction $\frac{a}{b}$ on a number line diagram by marking off a lengths $\frac{1}{b}$ from 0. Recognize that the resulting interval has size $\frac{a}{b}$ and that its endpoint locates the number $\frac{1}{b}$ on the number line.	Unit 4 Lessons 2, 3; Unit 5 Lesson 9
3.NF.A.3	Explain equivalence of fractions in special cases, and compare fractions by reasoning about their size.	Unit 4 Lessons 4, 5; Unit 5 Lessons 7, 8, 9, 10
3.NF.A.3.a	Understand two fractions as equivalent (equal) if they are the same size, or the same point on a number line.	Unit 5 Lessons 7, 8, 9, 10
3.NF.A.3.b	Recognize and generate simple equivalent fractions, e.g., $\frac{1}{2} = \frac{2}{4}, \frac{4}{6} = \frac{2}{3}$. Explain why the fractions are equivalent, e.g., by using a visual fraction model.	Unit 5 Lessons 7, 8, 9, 10
3.NF.A.3.c	Express whole numbers as fractions, and recognize fractions that are equivalent to whole numbers.	Unit 4 Lessons 3, 4; Unit 5 Lessons 8, 9
3.NF.A.3.d	Compare two fractions with the same numerator or the same denominator by reasoning about their size. Recognize that comparisons are valid only when the two fractions refer to the same whole. Record the results of comparisons with the symbols >, =, or <, and justify the conclusions, e.g., by using a visual fraction model.	Unit 3 Lessons 4, 5; Unit 5 Lessons 9, 10

3.MD Measurement and Data

Solve problems involving measurement and estimation of intervals of time, liquid volumes, and masses of objects.

3.MD.A.1	Tell and write time to the nearest minute and measure time intervals in minutes. Solve word problems involving addition and subtraction of time intervals in minutes, e.g., by representing the problem on a number line diagram.	Unit 4 Lessons 7; 8, 9, 10, 11, 16
3.MD.A.2	Measure and estimate liquid volumes and masses of objects using standard units of grams (g), kilograms (kg), and liters (l). Add, subtract, multiply, or divide to solve one-step word problems involving masses or volumes that are given in the same units, e.g., by using drawings (such as a beaker with a measurement scale) to represent the problem.	Unit 7 Lessons 1, 2, 3, 4

■ Major   ■ Supporting   ■ Additional

Represent and interpret data.

3.MD.B.3	Draw a scaled picture graph and a scaled bar graph to represent a data set with several categories. Solve one- and two-step "how many more" and "how many less" problems using information presented in scaled bar graphs.	Unit 4 Lessons 12, 13, 15
3.MD.B.4	Generate measurement data by measuring lengths using rulers marked with halves and fourths of an inch. Show the data by making a line plot, where the horizontal scale is marked off in appropriate units—whole numbers, halves, or quarters.	Unit 4 Lessons 6, 14, 15, 16

Geometric measurement: understand concepts of area and relate area to multiplication and to addition.

3.MD.C.5	Recognize area as an attribute of plane figures and understand concepts of area measurement.	Unit 1 Lesson 11; Unit 2 Lesson 2; Unit 5 Lessons 1, 3
3.MD.C.5.a	A square with side length 1 unit, called "a unit square," is said to have "one square unit" of area, and can be used to measure area.	Unit 1 Lesson 11; Unit 2 Lesson 2; Unit 5 Lessons 1, 3
3.MD.C.5.b	A plane figure that can be covered without gaps or overlaps by n unit squares is said to have an area of n square units.	Unit 1 Lesson 11; Unit 2 Lesson 2; Unit 5 Lessons 1, 3
3.MD.C.6	Measure areas by counting unit squares (square cm, square m, square in, square ft, and improvised units).	Unit 1 Lesson 11; Unit 5 Lessons 1, 2, 6
3.MD.C.7	Relate area to the operations of multiplication and addition.	Unit 1 Lesson 11, 12, 14; Unit 2 Lessons 2, 6, 8; Unit 5 Lessons 1, 2, 3, 4, 5; Unit 7 Lesson 9
3.MD.C.7.a	Find the area of a rectangle with whole-number side lengths by tiling it, and show that the area is the same as would be found by multiplying the side lengths.	Unit 1 Lesson 11; Unit 2 Lesson 2; Unit 5 Lessons 1, 2
3.MD.C.7.b	Multiply side lengths to find areas of rectangles with whole number side lengths in the context of solving real world and mathematical problems, and represent whole-number products as rectangular areas in mathematical reasoning.	Unit 1 Lessons 11, 12, 14; Unit 2 Lessons 2, 6; Unit 5 Lessons 1, 2, 3, 4, 5
3.MD.C.7.c	Use tiling to show in a concrete case that the area of a rectangle with whole-number side lengths a and b + c is the sum of a × b and a × c. Use area models to represent the distributive property in mathematical reasoning.	Unit 1 Lessons 11, 12, 14; Unit 5 Lesson 2
3.MD.C.7.d	Recognize area as additive. Find areas of rectilinear figures by decomposing them into non-overlapping rectangles and adding the areas of the non-overlapping parts, applying this technique to solve real world problems.	Unit 1 Lesson 11; Unit 2 Lessons 2, 6, 8; Unit 5 Lessons 2, 4, 5; Unit 7 Lesson 9

Geometric measurement: recognize perimeter as an attribute of plane figures and distinguish between linear and area measures.

3.MD.D.8	Solve real world and mathematical problems involving perimeters of polygons, including finding the perimeter given the side lengths, finding an unknown side length, and exhibiting rectangles with the same perimeter and different areas or with the same area and different perimeters.	Unit 5 Lessons 1, 2, 3, 5; Unit 7 Lesson 11

3.G Geometry

Reason with shapes and their attributes.

3.G.A.1	Understand that shapes in different categories (e.g., rhombuses, rectangles, and others) may share attributes (e.g., having four sides), and that the shared attributes can define a larger category (e.g., quadrilaterals). Recognize rhombuses, rectangles, and squares as examples of quadrilaterals, and draw examples of quadrilaterals that do not belong to any of these subcategories.	Unit 7 Lessons 5, 6, 7, 8, 9
3.G.A.2	Partition shapes into parts with equal areas. Express the area of each part as a unit fraction of the whole.	Unit 4 Lessons 1, 2; Unit 5 Lesson 10; Unit 7 Lesson 5

© Houghton Mifflin Harcourt Publishing Company

■ Major   ■ Supporting   ■ Additional

Common Core State Standards for Mathematical Practice

MP1 Make sense of problems and persevere in solving them.

Mathematically proficient students start by explaining to themselves the meaning of a problem and looking for entry points to its solution. They analyze givens, constraints, relationships, and goals. They make conjectures about the form and meaning of the solution and plan a solution pathway rather than simply jumping into a solution attempt. They consider analogous problems, and try special cases and simpler forms of the original problem in order to gain insight into its solution. They monitor and evaluate their progress and change course if necessary. Older students might, depending on the context of the problem, transform algebraic expressions or change the viewing window on their graphing calculator to get the information they need. Mathematically proficient students can explain correspondences between equations, verbal descriptions, tables, and graphs or draw diagrams of important features and relationships, graph data, and search for regularity or trends. Younger students might rely on using concrete objects or pictures to help conceptualize and solve a problem. Mathematically proficient students check their answers to problems using a different method, and they continually ask themselves, "Does this make sense?" They can understand the approaches of others to solving complex problems and identify correspondences between different approaches.

Unit 1 Lessons 3, 4, 5, 6, 7, 9, 10, 12, 13, 14, 16, 18, 19
Unit 2 Lessons 1, 2, 4, 7, 9, 10, 11, 13, 15
Unit 3 Lessons 3, 4, 5, 6, 7, 8, 9, 10, 11, 12, 13, 14, 15, 16, 17, 18
Unit 4 Lessons 7, 9, 11, 12, 13, 14, 15, 16
Unit 5 Lessons 2, 5
Unit 6 Lessons 1, 2, 3, 4, 6, 7, 8, 9, 10, 11
Unit 7 Lessons 1, 2, 3, 4, 9

MP2 Reason abstractly and quantitatively.

Mathematically proficient students make sense of quantities and their relationships in problem situations. They bring two complementary abilities to bear on problems involving quantitative relationships: the ability to decontextualize—to abstract a given situation and represent it symbolically and manipulate the representing symbols as if they have a life of their own, without necessarily attending to their referents—and the ability to contextualize, to pause as needed during the manipulation process in order to probe into the referents for the symbols involved. Quantitative reasoning entails habits of creating a coherent representation of the problem at hand; considering the units involved; attending to the meaning of quantities, not just how to compute them; and knowing and flexibly using different properties of operations and objects.

Unit 1 Lessons 1, 2, 3, 5, 6, 7, 8, 10, 11, 12, 19
Unit 2 Lessons 1, 2, 3, 5, 6, 8, 13, 15
Unit 3 Lessons 1, 2, 5, 6, 9, 11, 12, 13, 14, 15, 16, 17, 18
Unit 4 Lessons 1, 2, 3, 4, 6, 9, 13, 14, 16
Unit 5 Lessons 1, 2, 3, 4, 5, 7, 8, 9, 10
Unit 6 Lessons 1, 2, 3, 4, 8, 11
Unit 7 Lessons 1, 2, 3, 5, 9

Common Core State Standards for Mathematical Practice

MP3 Construct viable arguments and critique the reasoning of others.

Mathematically proficient students understand and use stated assumptions, definitions, and previously established results in constructing arguments. They make conjectures and build a logical progression of statements to explore the truth of their conjectures. They are able to analyze situations by breaking them into cases, and can recognize and use counterexamples. They justify their conclusions, communicate them to others, and respond to the arguments of others. They reason inductively about data, making plausible arguments that take into account the context from which the data arose. Mathematically proficient students are also able to compare the effectiveness of two plausible arguments, distinguish correct logic or reasoning from that which is flawed, and—if there is a flaw in an argument—explain what it is. Elementary students can construct arguments using concrete referents such as objects, drawings, diagrams, and actions. Such arguments can make sense and be correct, even though they are not generalized or made formal until later grades. Later, students learn to determine domains to which an argument applies. Students at all grades can listen or read the arguments of others, decide whether they make sense, and ask useful questions to clarify or improve the arguments.

Unit 1 Lessons 1, 2, 3, 4, 5, 6, 7, 8, 9, 10, 11, 12, 13, 14, 15, 16, 18, 19
Unit 2 Lessons 1, 2, 3, 4, 5, 6, 8, 9, 10, 11, 12, 13, 14, 15
Unit 3 Lessons 1, 2, 3, 4, 5, 6, 7, 8, 9, 10, 12, 13, 14, 15, 16, 17, 18
Unit 4 Lessons 1, 2, 3, 4, 5, 6, 7, 8, 9, 10, 11, 12, 13, 14, 15, 16
Unit 5 Lessons 1, 2, 3, 4, 5, 6, 7, 8, 9, 10
Unit 6 Lessons 1, 2, 3, 4, 5, 6, 7, 8, 9, 10, 11
Unit 7 Lessons 1, 2, 3, 4, 5, 6, 7, 8, 9

MP4 Model with mathematics.

Mathematically proficient students can apply the mathematics they know to solve problems arising in everyday life, society, and the workplace. In early grades, this might be as simple as writing an addition equation to describe a situation. In middle grades, a student might apply proportional reasoning to plan a school event or analyze a problem in the community. By high school, a student might use geometry to solve a design problem or use a function to describe how one quantity of interest depends on another. Mathematically proficient students who can apply what they know are comfortable making assumptions and approximations to simplify a complicated situation, realizing that these may need revision later. They are able to identify important quantities in a practical situation and map their relationships using such tools as diagrams, two-way tables, graphs, flowcharts and formulas. They can analyze those relationships mathematically to draw conclusions. They routinely interpret their mathematical results in the context of the situation and reflect on whether the results make sense, possibly improving the model if it has not served its purpose.

Unit 1 Lessons 1, 2, 3, 4, 5, 6, 7, 8, 9, 10, 12, 13, 14, 16, 18, 19
Unit 2 Lessons 2, 4, 7, 9, 11, 13, 15
Unit 3 Lessons 3, 4, 7, 8, 9, 10, 11, 12, 14, 17, 18
Unit 4 Lessons 3, 7, 9, 10, 11, 12, 13, 14, 16
Unit 5 Lessons 2, 5, 6, 9, 10
Unit 6 Lessons 1, 2, 3, 4, 8, 9, 10, 11
Unit 7 Lessons 1, 2, 3, 4, 9

■ Major ■ Supporting ■ Additional

© Houghton Mifflin Harcourt Publishing Company

MP5 Use appropriate tools strategically.

Mathematically proficient students consider the available tools when solving a mathematical problem. These tools might include pencil and paper, concrete models, a ruler, a protractor, a calculator, a spreadsheet, a computer algebra system, a statistical package, or dynamic geometry software. Proficient students are sufficiently familiar with tools appropriate for their grade or course to make sound decisions about when each of these tools might be helpful, recognizing both the insight to be gained and their limitations. For example, mathematically proficient high school students analyze graphs of functions and solutions generated using a graphing calculator. They detect possible errors by strategically using estimation and other mathematical knowledge. When making mathematical models, they know that technology can enable them to visualize the results of varying assumptions, explore consequences, and compare predictions with data. Mathematically proficient students at various grade levels are able to identify relevant external mathematical resources, such as digital content located on a website, and use them to pose or solve problems. They are able to use technological tools to explore and deepen their understanding of concepts.

Unit 1 Lessons 1, 2, 3, 4, 5, 6, 7, 8, 9, 10, 11, 12, 13, 14, 15, 16, 17, 18, 19
Unit 2 Lessons 1, 2, 3, 4, 5, 6, 7, 8, 9, 10, 11, 12, 13, 14, 15
Unit 3 Lessons 1, 2, 3, 4, 5, 6, 7, 8, 13, 17, 18
Unit 4 Lessons 1, 2, 3, 5, 6, 7, 8, 9, 10, 14, 16
Unit 5 Lessons 1, 2, 6, 7, 8, 10
Unit 6 Lessons 1, 2, 3, 4, 11
Unit 7 Lessons 1, 2, 3, 5, 7, 8, 9

MP6 Attend to precision.

Mathematically proficient students try to communicate precisely to others. They try to use clear definitions in discussion with others and in their own reasoning. They state the meaning of the symbols they choose, including using the equal sign consistently and appropriately. They are careful about specifying units of measure, and labeling axes to clarify the correspondence with quantities in a problem. They calculate accurately and efficiently, express numerical answers with a degree of precision appropriate for the problem context. In the elementary grades, students give carefully formulated explanations to each other. By the time they reach high school they have learned to examine claims and make explicit use of definitions.

Unit 1 Lessons 1, 2, 3, 4, 5, 6, 7, 8, 9, 10, 11, 12, 13, 14, 15, 16, 18, 19
Unit 2 Lessons 1, 2, 3, 4, 5, 6, 7, 8, 9, 10, 11, 12, 13, 14, 15
Unit 3 Lessons 1, 2, 3, 4, 5, 6, 7, 8, 9, 10, 11, 12, 13, 14, 15, 16, 17, 18
Unit 4 Lessons 1, 2, 3, 4, 5, 6, 7, 8, 9, 10, 11, 12, 13, 14, 15, 16
Unit 5 Lessons 1, 2, 3, 4, 5, 6, 7, 8, 9, 10
Unit 6 Lessons 1, 2, 3, 4, 5, 6, 7, 8, 9, 10, 11
Unit 7 Lessons 1, 2, 3, 4, 5, 6, 7, 8, 9

MP7 Look for and make use of structure.

Mathematically proficient students look closely to discern a pattern or structure. Young students, for example, might notice that three and seven more is the same amount as seven and three more, or they may sort a collection of shapes according to how many sides the shapes have. Later, students will see 7×8 equals the well remembered $7 \times 5 + 7 \times 3$, in preparation for learning about the distributive property. In the expression $x^2 + 9x + 14$, older students can see the 14 as 2×7 and the 9 as $2 + 7$. They recognize the significance of an existing line in a geometric figure and can use the strategy of drawing an auxiliary line for solving problems. They also can step back for an overview and shift perspective. They can see complicated things, such as some algebraic expressions, as single objects or as being composed of several objects. For example, they can see $5 - 3(x - y)^2$ as 5 minus a positive number times a square and use that to realize that its value cannot be more than 5 for any real numbers x and y.

Unit 1 Lessons 1, 2, 4, 5, 6, 7, 8, 10, 11, 12, 13, 15, 19
Unit 2 Lessons 1, 3, 5, 6, 14, 15
Unit 3 Lessons 1, 2, 3, 4, 11, 14, 16, 17,
Unit 4 Lessons 1, 2, 3, 16
Unit 5 Lessons 2, 4. 6. 7, 10
Unit 6 Lessons 1, 2, 3, 4, 5, 8, 11
Unit 7 Lessons 1, 5, 6, 7, 8, 9

MP8 Look for and express regularity in repeated reasoning.

Mathematically proficient students notice if calculations are repeated, and look both for general methods and for shortcuts. Upper elementary students might notice when dividing 25 by 11 that they are repeating the same calculations over and over again, and conclude they have a repeating decimal. By paying attention to the calculation of slope as they repeatedly check whether points are on the line through (1, 2) with slope 3, middle school students might abstract the equation $(y - 2)/(x - 1) = 3$. Noticing the regularity in the way terms cancel when expanding $(x - 1)(x + 1)$, $(x - 1)(x^2 + x + 1)$, and $(x - 1)(x^3 + x^2 + x + 1)$ might lead them to the general formula for the sum of a geometric series. As they work to solve a problem, mathematically proficient students maintain oversight of the process, while attending to the details. They continually evaluate the reasonableness of their intermediate results.

Unit 1 Lessons 1, 2, 3, 5, 7, 8, 10, 11, 12, 19
Unit 2 Lessons 1, 2, 3, 5, 6, 10, 12, 14, 15
Unit 3 Lessons 5, 6, 14, 17, 18
Unit 4 Lessons 1, 2, 3, 5, 6, 15, 16
Unit 5 Lessons 3, 6, 7, 10
Unit 6 Lessons 1, 4, 9, 11
Unit 7 Lessons 8, 9

■ Major ■ Supporting ■ Additional

A

**Addend, 355, 359–360. *See also*
Addition.**
  multidigit, 203–205, 206–207, 208–210, 225
  representing unknown, 360
  unknown, 359–360

Addition, 203, 361–362
  equations, 147, 358
  estimate sums, 196, 383–384
  Fluency Check, 95, 278, 344, 377, 418, 441
  models
    Equations, 358
    Math Mountains, 355, 359–360, 364
    Proof Drawings, 203–206
  multidigit addends, 203–205, 206–207, 208–210, 225
  problem types
    Add To, 356
    Put Together/Take Apart, 356
  Properties
    Associative Property, 73
    Commutative, 73
    Identity Property, 73
  relate to subtraction, 221–222
  strategies
    grouping, 203–205, 206–207
    New Groups Above method, 203
    New Groups Below method, 203
    Show All Totals method, 203
    using drawings, 203–205, 206
  time on a number line, 273
  vertical format, 206
  word problems, 203–205, 208, 209–210, 225, 226, 356, 359, 362–363

Algebra
  equations
    expressing relationships, 358
    modeling equations, 358
    situation equation and solution equations, 145–146, 365–366
    solving multiplication and division equations, 28, 36, 37, 74, 121–122, 365–366
    using a symbol to represent an unknown, 37, 121–122
    using a variable to represent an unknown, 37, 360, 365–366
    writing equations, 121–122, 146, 154, 171, 313–314, 365–366, 383–388
    writing related equations, 24, 26, 36
  expression, 358
  functions
    finding and writing the rule, 10
    function tables, 10
    using a rule, 10
  inverse operations
    multiplication and division, 23–26
  meaning of equality, 358
  order of operations, 149–150
  patterns. *See* Patterns.
  Properties
    Associative Property of addition, 73
    Associative Property of multiplication, 72–73
    Commutative Property of multiplication, 22, 73, 155
    Distributive Property, 55, 56, 60–61, 67–68, 313–314
    Identity Property of addition, 73
    Identity Property of multiplication, 73
    using Associative and Commutative Properties to solve problems, 72–74
    Zero Property, 72–73
  variables, 37, 365–366

Algorithms
  addition
    New Groups Above method, 203
    New Groups Below method, 203
    Show All Totals method, 203

Angles
  classifying triangles by, 422, 424
  naming, 421
  types of, 421

Area
  by counting, 112, 312
  Distributive Property, 55, 56, 60–61, 67, 313–314

D

Index

equations, 36, 121–122, 135–142, 147

Fluency Check, 212, 232, 344, 377, 392, 418, 441

model

  equal shares drawings, 24, 61

Product Cards, 167D, 167B, 167F, 167H, 167J

relate to multiplication, 23–26

square numbers, 125–128

Strategy Cards, 55K–55Z

unknown factor, 24, 361–362

word problems, 32, 45, 67–68, 75–76, 79–80, 91–92, 119–120, 133–134, 365

  writing, 38

Division Blockout Game, 131

Division Race Game, 82

Division Race Game Board, 84

Division Rule for Zero, 72

Divisor, 23

zero as, 72

Doubles

products of, 170

E

Equal groups, 7–10

Equality, meaning of, 358

Equal parts

unit fractions, 243–247

Equal Shares drawings, 8–9, 21–22, 24, 61

Equal sign (=), 358

Equation, 6, 365–366, 383–384

for area of rectangle, 313–314

expressing relationships, 358

relationship to Math Mountains, 355

situation equation and solution equations, 365–366

solving addition and subtraction equations, 207–210, 358, 359, 364

solving equations by using inverse operations, 23–26

solving multiplication and division equations, 52, 74, 75, 79–80, 121–122, 135–142, 362–363

using a symbol to represent an unknown, 23–26, 37, 121–122

using a variable to represent an unknown, 37, 360, 365–366

writing, 37, 45, 74, 75, 121–122, 146, 171, 358, 360, 365–366, 383–388

writing related equations, 24–26, 36, 52

Equivalent fractions, 335–338

Estimate, 195

capacity, 404

to check answers, 196, 198, 383–384

differences, 196

to find reasonable answers, 196–199, 383–384

length, 258

liquid volume, 404

to the nearest hundred, 195–196, 198, 199

to the nearest ten, 197–198

number of objects, 200

quantities, 200

sums, 196, 198, 209–210, 383–384

using rounding, 195–200, 383–384

weight and mass, 411, 414

Even numbers, 28

resulting products of, 170

Expanded form, 189, 193

Expression, 358

evaluate by using order of operations, 149–150

F

Factor, 6, 361–362, 365–366. *See also* **Multiplication, by 0, 1, 2, 3, 4, 5, 6, 7, 8, 9, 10**

Family Letter, 1–4, 11–14, 105–106, 183–186, 241–242, 263–264, 279–280, 307–308, 354–355, 401–402, 419–420

Fast array drawings, 46, 118, 124

Fluency Check. *See* **Addition; Assessment; Division; Multiplication; Subtraction.**

Focus on Mathematical Practices, 93–94, 171–172, 229–230, 295–296, 341–342, 389–390, 439

Index

Less than symbol (<), 367

Line plot, 259–260

generate data with halves and fourths, 259, 292, 296

making, 260, 292, 296

reading and interpreting, 291, 294

Line segment, 257–258

Liquid Volume (Capacity), 415

customary units, 403–406

estimate, 404

metric units, 407–408

using drawings to solve problems, 405–406

M

Manipulatives

base ten blocks, 155

Check Sheets

0s10s, 130

1s and 0s, 77–78

2s, 5s, 9s, and 10s, 43–44

3s and 4s, 57–58

5s and 2s, 29–30

6s, 7s, and 8s, 129

6s and 8s, 115–116

7s and squares, 125–126

10s and 9s, 39–40

clocks (analog), 265A–265B

Dashes, 85–90, 137–142, 157–162

Dash Record Sheet, 16

Division Race Game Board, 84

Fraction Circles, 255A–255B

Fraction Rectangles, 243A–243B

Fraction Strips, 335A–335B

High Card Wins, 66

multiplication tables (Targets), 31

Paper Clock, 265A–265B

perimeter and area, 311A–311B

Product Cards, 167A–267J

Quadrilaterals for Sorting, 439A–439B

Rulers, 257

Save the Stack, 65

Secret Code Cards, 189A–189D, 189A–189D

Signature Sheet, 15

Strategy Cards, 55A–55Z

Study Sheets, 17–18, 53–54, 109–110

Tangram Shapes, 327A–327B

Three-in-a-Row Game Grids, 83, 166

Triangles to Build Quadrilaterals and Polygons, 425A–425B, 427A–427B

Mass, 411–414, 416

estimate, 414

units of, 411–412

Math Journal, 19, 46, 120, 217

Math Mountain

relate addition and subtraction, 355, 359–360, 364

relationship to equations, 355, 364

total, 364

unknown number, 359–360

Math Tools. *See also* Equation; Math Mountain.

drawings and equations, 24

fast-array drawings, 46

Quick 9s multiplication and division, 41–42

represent word problems, 357

Measurement. *See also* Estimate; Time.

area

on a dot array, 309–310

of a rectangle, 112–114, 309–314, 439

square units, 112, 309–311, 439

centimeter, 309–310

choosing appropriate unit, 409, 411

generate data for line plots, 259, 292, 296

inch, 257–258, 259

length

customary units, 256–257

estimate, 258

liquid volume (capacity), 415

customary units, 403–406

estimate, 404

measure, 403–408

metric units, 407–408

using drawings, 405–406

mass, 416

estimate, 414

perimeter

on a dot array, 309–310

© Houghton Mifflin Harcourt Publishing Company

N

Index

Number line
addition and subtraction of time
intervals, 273–274
compare fractions on, 254
identify and locate fractions on a,
248–254, 337–338
representing measurement problems,
409–410

Numbers. *See* **Whole numbers.**

O

Octagons, 426
Odd numbers, 28
resulting products of, 28
Order numbers, 367
Order of operations, 149–150
Origami. *See* **Paper folding.**

P

Paper Clock, 265A–265B
Paper folding, 341–342
Parallelogram, 427–429
drawing, 431–433
rectangle, 312–326, 428–429, 432,
435–438
rhombus, 428–429, 433, 435–438
square, 428–429, 433, 435–438
**Path to Fluency, 10, 17, 19, 25, 27, 29,
31, 35, 39–41, 49–51, 53, 55, 57–61,
65–67, 72–74, 77–78, 81–82, 93–94, 96,
108–111, 115, 117–118, 120, 123–127,
129–133, 135–142, 157–160, 164–165,
167, 168–170, 174, 202–204, 212, 213,
215–221, 225, 232, 278, 298, 344, 358,
377, 392, 418, 441**
Patterns
count-bys and multiplication, 27, 31, 35,
42, 49–51, 60, 107, 115–117, 123,
169–170
on a multiplication table, 31, 128,
169–170
square numbers, 125–128

Pentagons, 426
Performance Task. *See* **Unit
Performance Task.**
Perimeter
on a dot array, 309–310
find unknown side lengths, 315–316
of a rectangle or square, 309–310,
315–316, 439
rectangles with same area and different
perimeter, 318
rectangles with same perimeter and
different area, 317
Pictograph
key, 281
making, 282
problem solving with, 28, 172, 281, 282,
285
reading and interpreting, 28, 172, 281,
282, 285
Place value
to add and subtract multidigit numbers,
203–205, 209–210
to round, 199
through hundreds, 187
through thousands, 188
in word problems, 192, 196, 203–206
**Place value drawings, 187–188, 193,
213–217**
circles, 187, 188, 213–217
hundred-box, 187, 213–217
ten-stick, 187, 213–217
thousand-bar, 188, 216
Plane figures. *See* **Geometry,
two-dimensional figures.**
Polygon. *See also* **Geometry.**
building from triangles, 425A–425B,
427A–427B
concave and convex, 425
naming, 426
quadrilateral
building, 425A–425B, 426
different shapes, 434
naming, 435
parallelogram, 427

Q

Index

Index

Z

Multiplication Table and Scrambled Tables (Volume 2)

E

×	4	2	5	1	3	8	10	7	9	6
4	16	8	20	4	12	32	40	28	36	24
1	4	2	5	1	3	8	10	7	9	6
2	8	4	10	2	6	16	20	14	18	12
5	20	10	25	5	15	40	50	35	45	30
3	12	6	15	3	9	24	30	21	27	18
9	36	18	45	9	27	72	90	63	81	54
6	24	12	30	6	18	48	60	42	54	36
10	40	20	50	10	30	80	100	70	90	60
7	28	14	35	7	21	56	70	49	63	42
8	32	16	40	8	24	64	80	56	72	48

F

×	9	8	6	7	4	6	8	7	4	9
2	18	16	12	14	8	12	16	14	8	18
3	27	24	18	21	12	18	24	21	12	27
5	45	40	30	35	20	30	40	35	20	45
3	27	24	18	21	12	18	24	21	12	27
5	45	40	30	35	20	30	40	35	20	45
9	81	72	54	63	36	54	72	63	36	81
7	63	56	42	49	28	42	56	49	28	63
6	54	48	36	42	24	36	48	42	24	54
8	72	64	48	56	32	48	64	56	32	72
4	36	32	24	28	16	24	32	28	16	36

G

×	7	6	8	7	8	6	8	7	6	8
5	35	30	40	35	40	30	40	35	30	40
4	28	24	32	28	32	24	32	28	24	32
3	21	18	24	21	24	18	24	21	18	24
2	14	12	16	14	16	12	16	14	12	16
8	56	48	64	56	64	48	64	56	48	64
9	63	54	72	63	72	54	72	63	54	72
7	49	42	56	49	56	42	56	49	42	56
6	42	36	48	42	48	36	48	42	36	48
8	56	48	64	56	64	48	64	56	48	64
6	42	36	48	42	48	36	48	42	36	48

H

×	4	6	7	8	9	6	9	8	7	4
4	16	24	28	32	36	24	36	32	28	16
6	24	36	42	48	54	36	54	48	42	24
7	28	42	49	56	63	42	63	56	49	28
8	32	48	56	64	72	48	72	64	56	32
9	36	54	63	72	81	54	81	72	63	36
8	32	48	56	64	72	48	72	64	56	32
9	36	54	63	72	81	54	81	72	63	36
4	16	24	28	32	36	24	36	32	28	16
7	28	42	49	56	63	42	63	56	49	28
6	24	36	42	48	54	36	54	48	42	24

Be an Illustrator

Illustrator: Josh Brill

Did you ever try to use shapes to draw animals like the moose on the cover?

Over the last 10 years Josh has been using geometric shapes to design his animals. His aim is to keep the animal drawings simple and use color to make them appealing.

Add some color to the moose Josh drew. Then try drawing a cat or dog or some other animal using the shapes below.

Shape Toolbox